Exploring Shakespeare

Julius Caesar

Approaches and activities

Brenda Pinder

Oxford University Press 1994

Oxford University Press, Walton Street, Oxford OX2 6DP

Oxford New York Toronto
Delhi Bombay Calcutta Madras Karachi
Kuala Lumpur Singapore Hong Kong Tokyo
Nairobi Dar es Salaam Cape Town
Melbourne Auckland Madrid

and associate companies in
Berlin Ibadan

Oxford is a trade mark of Oxford University Press

Introduction © Susan Leach 1994
Ways In, The Play and Overview © Brenda Pinder 1994

Published by Oxford University Press 1994

A CIP catalogue record for this book is available from the British Library

ISBN 0 19 831288 1

Printed in Great Britain at the University Press, Cambridge

Acknowledgements

The cover illustration is by Anthea Toorchen.

The inside illustrations are by Jonathon Heap pp. 23, 44, 47, 53, 78, 86; and
John Walker pp. 20, 24, 28. The handwriting is by Elitta Fell.

The publishers would like to thank the following for permission to reproduce
photographs:

The Marquess of Bath p. 82; Donald Cooper Photostage pp. 19, 30, 41, 50, 69
both, 83 both; The Billy Rose Theater Collection, N.Y Public Library at Lincoln
Center, Astor, Lenox & Tilden Foundations, p. 84.

Contents

Introduction

The *Exploring Shakespeare* series	*4*
Introduction to active approaches	*6*
Ways in	*13*

The play

Act 1 scene 1	*19*
Act 1 scene 2	*21*
Act 1 scene 3	*27*
Act 2 scene 1	*30*
Act 2 scene 2	*34*
Act 2 scenes 3 and 4	*37*
Act 3 scene 1	*39*
Act 3 scene 2	*45*
Act 3 scene 3	*49*
Act 4 scene 1	*51*
Act 4 scenes 2 and 3	*52*
Act 5 scene 1	*56*
Act 5 scenes 2 and 3	*58*
Act 5 scenes 4 and 5	*60*

Overview

Characters	*67*
Plot	*76*
Language and verse	*79*
Themes and ideas	*82*

Introduction

The *Exploring Shakespeare* series

These student study books to accompany *Romeo and Juliet, A Midsummer Night's Dream,* and *Julius Caesar* are intended primarily for Year 9 students working towards KS3 of the National Curriculum in English.

As they all offer a wide range of activities they can also be used with other secondary students, particularly those in years 10 and 11 working towards GCSE English and English (Literature).

The general purpose of the books is to enable the inexperienced student, probably coming to Shakespeare for the first time, to make sense of the plays from the start, and to find enjoyment in reading and working on them. We also hope that students' self-confidence in tackling Shakespeare will grow as a result of using these books, and that they will go on with enthusiasm to read and enjoy other plays by Shakespeare.

Each of the three books mirrors the individuality of its author, as well as reflecting a common approach to the study of the plays, based on active, collaborative work. The differences between the three books also reflect the very different natures of the three plays; however common the approach, each play demands its own separate treatment.

The books follow a common format:
1   An Introduction to Active Approaches, aimed at the teacher, which provides a simple explanation of the active approaches used across all three books; and a Ways In section, which offers students ideas for introductory work on the plays, before full study is begun. For students who already know the basic plot and characters, some of these suggestions will be redundant.
2   Activities on the play itself, scene by scene.
3   An Overview section, which offers activities to help students look back at the plays and consider them as complete entities, from a variety of viewpoints related to themes, imagery, language, characters, and plot.

The second section, of scene-by-scene activities on the play, requires a little more clarification. It has been organized so that usually more than one activity is offered for each scene. It is assumed that teachers will not work through these activities from start to finish, but will select assignments from the range on offer.

Scenes are prefaced by a brief resumé of their importance to the play, with an indication of their time and place. *Exploring Shakespeare: Romeo and Juliet* makes most obvious reference to time, with fewer specific references in *A Midsummer Night's Dream*. *Julius Caesar* is concerned with only a few salient calendar dates, and assumes the passing of time without mentioning it, so this has few specific references.

Where an activity refers to specific lines of text within a scene, a line reference is given, based on the *Oxford School Shakespeare* edition of the play.

Activities which require a cleared space for students to work in are marked in the text with an icon ▨. These activities are often the most challenging for the teacher to organize and oversee, so they may not be the first choice of teachers who are still 'finding their Shakespeare feet'!

Scene-by-scene activities are based on approaches designed to fulfil several purposes:

- to enable students to engage with the underlying concerns of the plays
- to encourage students to think for themselves, and be prepared to offer their own ideas and conclusions
- to help students work independently of direct supervision by the teacher, alone, in pairs, and in groups
- to take students into a deeper knowledge and understanding of the plays than is implied by the narrow requirements of KS3 SATs.

The activities suggested throughout the scene-by-scene pages include acting, improvisation, mime, freeze frames, and other use of voice and movement; written, visual/illustrative and stage/theatrical assignments; discussion, hotseating, and inquests; and searching and researching. The emphasis throughout is on taking on the language of the plays as it stands – on using its differences and challenges positively and creatively.

We suggest that students have a journal, log, or notebook for the written activities, especially for those which ask them to note down their thoughts or reactions. (Sometimes the word 'journal' is used in the students' books.)

These books can be used in different ways to fit in with students' previous experience. Where students have already read the play, or seen a film version of the play, the activities will help them explore the play in greater depth, and with help, consolidate what they already know. Where students are coming to the play for the first time, it is possible to run the student study book alongside the reading of the play. The preferred approach will need to be thought through by the teacher. Each way of using these students' books will produce different results and reactions in the classroom.

Assignments in the scene-by-scene sections make clear how students should be grouped, and sometimes suggest that they should get their teacher to help them. It has been taken for granted that teachers will set up each lesson, but the emphasis is always on students doing these assignments for themselves. They are consistently addressed as 'you' in active collaboration with each other.

Introduction to active approaches

Many of the active approaches used in these books are already well-established as good classroom practice, while others are based on techniques developed by theatre practitioners.

Reading

Because students coming new to Shakespeare are unfamiliar with Shakespeare's language and verse form, it is useful to have a range of reading techniques at hand to help them grasp the meaning of the texts. The reading techniques described below emphasize particular features of different kinds of text. All the techniques can be used with pairs, groups, or whole classes. They are designed to involve all students in reading. Success with these techniques depends on all students using the same edition of the play, because of variations in punctuation between editions.

It is advisable to try out all these reading techniques with a class, so that students know how to use them when working independently.

Reading by punctuation marks

Have students seated in a large circle if possible. They read in turns round the group, each person stopping and handing on to the next person at a punctuation mark.

Reading by punctuation marks makes long speeches in blank verse manageable for students, and helps them grasp the ideas and development of thought in a speech. The words between punctuation marks express one idea or thought, even the word 'and': every speech moves from an opening statement, question, or proposition to another position. The technique highlights single words and images, and helps students identify metaphor and imagery. Many assignments which ask students to find key words and images, thoughts and feelings in the text depend on this reading technique.

Where students are using this technique in a pair or a small group, the same method applies.

Reading by 'sense units' (usually marked off by full stops, semicolons or the word 'and') is a variation of this. It invites students to ignore commas and read on until there is a sense 'pause', rather than having maybe only a single word to read.

Reading by sentences

This technique allows whole thoughts to be read/heard at once. The irregularity of sentence length in speeches and the linking of thoughts are clearly shown by using this method. A development of this is to write out each sentence separately to see how the thinking has moved on from one idea to the next. Some assignments build on this by asking students to headline the main thought in a sentence.

Reading by speeches

Many scenes in the plays work best with one person reading the whole of any speech, and the next person reading the next speech, and so on round the group. This retains whole group involvement, without burdening individuals with the responsibility for 'parts'. It allows the cohesion of each character's words to be taken in, and is a good technique to use when whole scenes are being read in which no character speaks more than about six lines at once.

A mixture of all techniques can be used in any speech or scene; it is a good idea to vary these approaches when working on any part of the plays.

Classroom organization

All these techniques can be used in the classroom, by students sitting at desks or at groups of desks. This is not ideal, but at least all are participating and experiencing the text. The focus here would be on reading and listening.

A space allowing students to sit in a circle encourages more collaborative participation: it focuses attention on the text and on each student in turn, and emphasizes the importance of each individual's contribution.

A space allowing physical movement offers the greatest possibilities. Physicalizing techniques can be used here, marrying physical movement with one or more reading techniques.

Physical work

The following suggestions for physical ways of working on the plays are not all explicitly included in the activities in the book. They are offered here, in outline, for the teacher who may wish to go beyond static reading of the texts, but who does not want students to 'act it out' yet. In all of them, it is assumed that the teacher will be working with a whole class, or large group. The use of the reading techniques described above is implied in these physical activities.

By involving physical movement, these techniques:
■ make clear that this is the language of theatre, to be spoken out loud
■ release the potential energy of the words, and allow students to experience the power of the language.

Moving to the words

■ Students walk, or run, round the room, reading the chosen piece of text aloud all together. They change direction at every punctuation point, or every sentence, or every end of line. Choose a speed and type of movement to help students experience the energy and rhythms of the verse.

■ The teacher, facing the students standing in their own space in the room, reads the lines aloud, divided into 'sense units'; students repeat the words, and 'show' their meaning at the same time. For example, as they repeat the words, 'Gallop apace, you fiery-footed steeds, towards Phoebus' lodging', for the first time, students might be expected to gallop, to indicate 'fiery steeds' in their movement, and to be puzzled by 'Phoebus' lodging'. Briefly explain 'Phoebus' lodging' and ask them to try again.

Assignments which ask students to visualize and illustrate images and meaning can be started off with this method.

■ Set up physical impediments to the readers. The idea is not to create chaos, but to 'challenge' readers into vocalizing the emotion and energy in the words. In several of these methods, students can be given a line to learn before the activity takes place, so they are not hampered by books as they move about. Some methods are:
a crowd in round one person reading the chosen speech, echoing key words pre-selected by the teacher
b make pairs pull against each other as they read a speech between them
c make one reader of the selected speech do some physical task, for example stacking books, moving from one chair to another on punctuation points
d allocate lines to groups at each end of the room; in order of the lines, students run across the room shouting out their words
e one person reads; one or more students try to stop him or her crossing the room.

More active reading

■ Use the chosen reading approach round the circle; each speaker turns to face the next to say their words.

- Use the chosen reading approach round the circle: each reader walks to the middle of the circle to say their words, if possible with an appropriate gesture to show their meaning.

- As one group of students reads the lines, other students are asked to echo and repeat key words and ideas.

- Vary the pace of any physical activity.

- Vary the volume in reading activities – ask students to use their voice control to whisper, shout, and make appropriate vocal sound effects.

- Work on the words in the verse whose meaning is entirely dependent on context, for example 'here', 'you', 'me', 'that', 'he', 'her', 'she'. These are known as *deictic* words.

Two people reading Paris's and Juliet's interchange –

> Paris: Do not deny to *him* that *you* love *me*.
> Juliet: *I* will confess to *you* that *I* love *him*.

– highlight these deictic words by pointing to themselves on 'I' and 'me', the other person on 'you', and at Friar Laurence (or an agreed spot in the room) on 'him'. Focusing like this on these words makes their meaning absolutely clear in the specific context. For more complex speeches or interchanges, involving reference to more than one other person, the room can be prepared by pinning up round the walls the names of these characters. As students read, they point to the relevant name, or themselves, on each deictic word. 'Here', 'there', 'up', 'down' and so on can also be treated in this way.

This treatment of deictic words will work whichever reading method has been chosen.

Further active approaches

Additional techniques can be used to increase students' knowledge and understanding of the text.

Acting/presentation

Some activities ask students to act out a scene or part of a scene. This is very useful for students with the confidence to do it, but for others a joint presentation can be preferable.

By using a combination of different reading and physical techniques, students can prepare presentations which involve everyone, without inhibiting those who dislike being 'on show' on their own. One example: in each group some students can be responsible for reading one part between them, while other students work out mimes to accompany the spoken words.

Mime

Mime is useful for students who have yet to gain the confidence to read aloud. It can be developed into 'dumbshow', a mimed presentation of the main action of a scene, or to show the actions of characters as described by others: for example, when Puck describes the flight of the Athenian workmen after Bottom appears with the ass's head; when Benvolio describes two of the street fights; when Casca describes Caesar being offered the crown.

Hotseating, interviewing, interrogating

In each of these activities, a student takes on the role of a character in the play and is questioned about that character's actions, motivation, and thoughts.

In **hotseating**, the whole class or group questions the character. This allows all students to become involved, although they may not all wish to participate.

In **interviewing**, a group or pair, with a specific purpose in mind (producing a newspaper report, television interview, radio interview, other write-up) interviews one person (or each other) in role as a character. Here, each person has a clearly defined part to play.

In **interrogation**, which can be done in groups or pairs, a student in role is put under duress, as in a real interrogation, about their part in the play. Good candidates for this treatment are Brutus, Cassius, and the Tribunes in *Julius Caesar*, Friar Laurence in *Romeo and Juliet*, Puck and Oberon in *A Midsummer Night's Dream*.

Inquest, court hearing

These are more formal frameworks for use when questioning characters, and are described fully where they occur in the activities on the play itself (pages 19–65).

Improvisation

Some assignments ask students to improvise

- the moments before a scene starts
- a similar situation to the one shown in a scene
- action described by a character but not seen on stage.

This can be linked to:

Freeze frames

(This is also know as tableaux, still photographs, or still images.)
In this method, students produce a static representation
designed to reveal the deeper meanings and significance of

- a moment in a scene
- the relationship between a group of characters
- what a character imagines
- images in the text.

Where it is used to represent a moment from a scene, students
can be asked to explain the thoughts and feelings of their
character, and the motivation behind their frozen stance at that
very moment.

Other activities

In addition to active reading techniques and physical activities,
the assignments included in this book offer a wide range of other
tasks intended to encourage and maintain the students'
engagement with the text.

These task are all described where they occur in the activities on
the play (pages 19–65), and include:

Written assignments

Students are invited to produce a wide range of written
responses to the texts. These are well-established in current
classroom practice (many of them can be found listed at the end
of the original Cox Report) and include letters, diaries, point-of-
view writing, accounts of events, students' own playscripts,
letters to and from an agony aunt, newspaper headlines, front
page reports and articles, stream-of-consciousness writing,
dossiers on characters, and obituaries.

Activities based on the play as theatre

Students are asked in some assignments to think about a part of the text as a piece to be staged, reminding them that the texts are above all plays for the theatre.

Students are invited to:
- design the stage set and costumes for a particular scene
- produce sound effects and tape them
- take the director's role, and make decisions about cutting, moving, or changing scenes or parts of scenes
- annotate a script with stage directions for the actors.

Text-based activities

These encourage students to look very closely at the text to:
- select single quotations which sum up whole speeches
- search through an act or the whole play for key images
- present a 'bare bones' or five-minute version of the play by stripping it down to essentials, still using the language of the play.

Showing and sharing

Finally, when students have completed an assignment, they are sometimes invited to share their work with other groups or with the whole class. When the work is active, requiring space and time, thought needs to be given to setting up the classroom for this, and to building in time for reflection, response, and reaction.

Ways in

Statues

Work in pairs, in as large a space as you can. One of you starts as the sculptor and the other is the statue. (This one has to be like a bendy rubber toy that stays in the positions it is put in.)

1   The sculptor moulds his or her clay person into a statue entitled 'Bravery'. When you've had a few minutes to do

this, all the sculptors should step back and have a look at everyone else's ideas.

2   Change over and the new sculptor makes a statue called 'Envy'. This is a bit more difficult but think how we show we are jealous by our way of standing, by our gestures, and by the expressions on our faces.

3   The first sculptor takes over again, and this time his or her creation is called 'Revenge'.

4   Another turn for the second sculptor, and an even harder statue to make – 'Ambition'.

5   Now make a sculpture with both of your bodies this time – called 'Assassination'.

6   Finally, join with another pair and create a tableau with your four bodies, to represent 'Conspiracy'.

Ask your teacher if you are not sure what any of the words mean.

Remember all these ideas if you can, as they are all present in the play you are about to study.

Improvisation

A group of schoolchildren has formed a gang, with a leader whom they now wish to change because the leader has turned out to be much too bossy and keeps telling everyone what to do. The members meet in secret, without the leader, to decide who should take over and how best to change from the old leader to the new one.

Working in groups of five or six, make up the scene of this meeting. Show what the members of the gang say and feel about their unwise choice of leader, and what they now plan to do. Rehearse your scene, then share yours with the others and watch theirs. Afterwards, discuss as a class the reasons why each of the groups wanted to get rid of their leader, and whether they chose the best means of doing it. How were they going to replace their leader? Could they be sure the new one would be any better? Would it be a good idea to change the leader at regular intervals, perhaps?

Group discussion

Julius Caesar raises some important and thought-provoking questions about leaders and leadership. Your group scene about choosing a new leader will have helped you start to think about some of these ideas.

Now discuss as a whole class your views on these questions:

- Is it ever right or justified to use violence to get rid of a leader? – for instance, a leader who takes more and more power, and acts more and more tyrannically; a leader who makes people desperate and won't allow them to voice their opinions; a leader who changes the rules after he or she has been chosen or elected, so people have no chance of choosing or electing a new ruler.
- What are the best ways of choosing or electing leaders?
- Do you think people need leaders at all?

Opening scene

Divide the whole class into two groups roughly equal in size: one to be 'Tribunes' and the other 'citizens'. Then give out the lines below round each group. Some people may end up with more than one line. In the left hand column are the Tribunes' lines, and in the right the citizens'.

1 Hence, home, you idle creatures, get you home!

2 What, know you not, being workmen, you must not walk on a working day without the sign of your profession?

3 Speak! What trade art thou?

    4 Why, sir, a carpenter.

5 Where is thy leather apron and thy rule?

6 What dost thou with thy best apparel on? You, sir, what trade are you?

    7 Truly, sir, I am but a cobbler.

8 But what trade, thou knave?

    9 A trade, sir, that he may use with a safe conscience – a mender of bad soles! (laughter from citizens)

10 What trade, thou knave, what trade?

11 I beseech you, sir, be not out with us. Yet if you are 'out' we can mend you! *(more laughter)*

12 What meanest thou by that? Mend me, saucy fellow?

13 Why, sir, cobble you! *(laughter again)*

14 You are cobblers then, are you?

15 We are indeed sir – surgeons to old shoes.

16 When they are in great danger, we re-cover them! *(more laughter)*

17 As proper men as ever trod on leather have gone upon our handiwork.

18 Wherefore are you not in your shop today? Why do you lead these men about the streets?

19 Truly, sir, to wear out their shoes – to get myself more work! *(more laughter from citizens)*

20 Indeed, sir, we make holiday to see Caesar and rejoice in his triumph.

21 Wherefore rejoice? What conquest brings he home?

22 You blocks, you stones, you worse than senseless things! O you hard hearts, you cruel men of Rome, knew you not Pompey?

23 What does he mean? Of course we knew Pompey!

24 Many a time and oft have you climbed up to walls and battlements, to towers and windows? Yes, to chimney-tops, your infants in your arms.

25 And there have sat the livelong day to see great Pompey pass the streets of Rome.

26 That's true; he's right, we have.

27 And do you now put on your best
    attire?

28 And do you now create a holiday?

29 And do you now strew flowers in
    his way, that comes in triumph over
    Pompey's blood?

    30 He's right; we shouldn't be rejoicing.

    31 Pompey's dead, that's true.

    32 Caesar's victory is Pompey's defeat.

    33 We forgot that. It's time we went home.

34 Be gone! Run to your houses, fall
    upon your knees, pray to the gods
    to forgive you for this ingratitude!

The little scene shows the citizens of Rome enjoying themselves because it is a holiday, so when they first come in they are laughing, joking, and perhaps chanting 'Caesar!' 'Caesar!' The Tribunes, who are the citizens' representatives in the Senate, are not in a holiday mood. They are angry at the quick and casual way the citizens have stopped supporting Pompey who was once joint leader with Caesar. The Tribunes stop the citizens and challenge them.

Now work on an acted version of the scene.

The numbers show the order in which the lines should be spoken. Before you start rehearsing, read through the whole scene round the class to get the feel of it, and then read it again to help you learn your cues and your lines. Your little performance will work much better if you know your lines.

Each person in each group needs to decide these things:
- What particular mood are you in? Does your line give you any clues?
- Who are you speaking to when you say your line?
- How will you react when others are speaking?

The Tribunes

Decide in your group what makes you so angry with the citizens, and whether anything they say at the beginning makes you laugh.

The citizens

Decide in your group what makes you laugh at the beginning: are the jokes really funny? Decide what makes you start taking things more seriously, and when you change mood.

Put your performance together in stages:

1   Have the two groups on opposite sides of the room saying the lines in turn.

2   Bring the groups close together, facing each other over an imaginary line.

3   Start moving about as you speak, remembering what you decided earlier about your own performance.

4   Pick up your cues as quickly as you can.

Your teacher may help you with your rehearsals. When you are ready, put on your final performance, which you could also tape-record if you like.

Discuss with your teacher what you have learned about:
■   the citizens
■   the Tribunes
■   the situation in Rome at the beginning of the play.

By being part of one of these two opposing groups, and by 'walking about inside the words', you will have grasped a great deal about *Julius Caesar*.

The play

Morning: the Feast of Lupercal, 15 February. A street in Rome. In this opening scene the ordinary people are celebrating Caesar's victory over Pompey. They are stopped by the Tribunes who remind them that not so long ago they were rejoicing over Pompey's triumph, so they slink off ashamed. The scene shows just how fickle the common people can be, to prepare the audience for what is to happen later.

Citizen's voice   *lines 1–63*

Look at the mood of the citizens when they come in. At first they are cheeky to the Tribunes with their puns (word-play) about 're-covering' shoes, as a surgeon might help a patient to 'recover'. There are some other puns here, too; see if you can spot them (lines 18, 20, and 24). When the Tribunes tell them off for their behaviour, they have nothing more to say.

Which lines spoken by the Tribunes have the greatest effect on them? Can you work out where they show how ashamed they are? Discuss your ideas with a partner, and then with your teacher.

Working on your own, imagine you are one of these citizens. After your return home you write down what your thoughts and feelings were while all this was going on. You might start with: 'We weren't doing any harm. We just wanted to celebrate – and these two Tribunes had to interfere . . .'

Working with a partner, use these thoughts as a basis for a little scene in which one of you is the returning citizen and the other a friend who questions you about what happened. Perform your scene to the class.

Police state?   *lines 66–78*

WANTED

FLAVIUS   MARULLUS

THESE MEN ARE DANGEROUS!
(Any information leading to their arrest
will be rewarded)

Today, we would probably think of speaking against the government as one of our democratic rights, but in many other countries, and in Caesar's Rome, this is not the case.

Later in the play we learn that Flavius and Marullus have been 'put to silence' for what they did to Caesar's statues.

Do you think their actions were enough to justify the authorities in doing this? What exactly were Flavius and Marullus planning to do? Why? See if you can find out from their speeches. (Flavius explains why in his last speech of the scene, lines 71–78.) Make brief notes about these points to use for your next activity.

Look at the 'Wanted' poster for the Tribunes Flavius and Marullus on page 20, and produce your own version of it.

You could draw the 'mug shots' yourself or cut out pictures from a newspaper or magazine. Add more information about what they are wanted for, where they were last seen, and anything else that might help lead to their arrest.

Working with a partner, imagine that one of these Tribunes has been caught and is being interrogated by Caesar's Secret Police. One of you should play the Tribune and the other the police officer questioning him. Prepare the questions likely to be asked by the police officer and the answers given by the Tribune. You might include questions about why he took down the decorations on the statues, what happened when he met the citizens, and what the two Tribunes said to the citizens. Think up other likely questions, and then rehearse your interrogation scene.

When you are ready, show your interrogation to another pair and watch theirs.

Act 1 scene 2

Later the same day. A public place in Rome.
Caesar appears for the first time. This man, hero-worshipped by the citizens, is clearly superstitious and by no means a superman. Cassius reminds Brutus of Caesar's weaknesses and tries hard to get him to join the conspiracy to assassinate Caesar. Casca reports to the two of them that Antony has offered a crown to Caesar but that he has refused it. The crowd, Casca says, are delighted as they wish him to be king but are pleased he

seems so modest and unwilling to snatch at power. Yet Casca thinks Caesar really wanted it.
Left alone at the end of the scene, Cassius shows that he is planning to persuade Brutus into his plot.

Superstitions and omens

What kind of superstitions do people follow today? Do you know anyone who won't walk under a ladder? Or who throws salt over their shoulder if any is spilt? Jot down three or four more superstitions that you have heard about.

The Romans took superstition a good deal more seriously than many people do today and they had lots of ways of finding out if a proposed action would turn out well. They called this investigating the 'omens', and one way of doing it was to cut open a recently-killed animal and look into its internal organs for any special signs or anything unusual.

They also believed that storms and any unnatural events were signs of some disaster – especially the death of a great man. (Note this down for your work later in the play.)

Almost as soon as Caesar appears in the play, he shows that he is superstitious by asking Antony to touch his wife, Calphurnia, as he runs past her in the ceremonial race that begins the Lupercal festivities. It was the belief of the time that a barren woman who had been touched by a runner in these festivities would then be able to have children. Perhaps Caesar is anxious to have an heir?

Caesar's weaknesses   *lines 90–131*

Besides his superstition, other signs of Caesar's weakness are seen. Cassius tells two stories in his speech (lines 90–131) specially to show that Caesar is far from the superman that some of the common people believe him to be. The story which starts at line 98 tells of a swimming challenge which Cassius won. What is he trying to prove by this tale, do you think? Note down your ideas.

Look at lines 119–128 for the next story, and note down what this one shows about Caesar.

Further on, in line 212, Caesar is shown to be a bit deaf, and then, later, in Casca's account of what happened offstage in the Forum, we hear that Caesar collapsed: he has the 'falling sickness' – epilepsy.

So it does look as if Shakespeare wants to show that Caesar is an ordinary man with many human weaknesses.

Use the diagram of the scales to 'weigh up' what you have found out so far about Caesar. Copy it and put into one half the weaknesses so far revealed and into the other anything you can think of that shows strength of character. There are a few ideas already there to start you off: see if you can complete it.

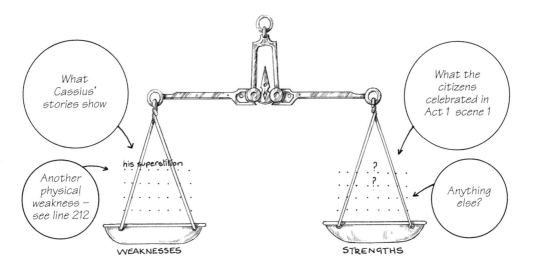

What Cassius' stories show

Another physical weakness – see line 212

his superstition

What the citizens celebrated in Act 1 scene 1

Anything else?

?
?
?

WEAKNESSES   STRENGTHS

Dossier on Cassius

Caesar says right from the beginning that he doesn't trust Cassius:

> Yond Cassius has a lean and hungry look;
> He thinks too much: such men are dangerous.
> (lines 193–4)

A modern ruler, with the kind of power Caesar had, would get his Secret Police to compile a dossier on Caius Cassius.

Imagine that Caesar has told his Secret Police to investigate Caius Cassius as a possible enemy of the State. They compile a secret dossier on him. Make up your version of their secret report for Caesar.

It would need to contain: name, address, age, appearance, distinguishing features (by which he could be easily recognized), places where he might be seen, and his friends. It could include information they have gathered by putting a 'tail' on him (having him followed). Perhaps it would also contain a character analysis so they could predict his likely behaviour in certain circumstances. Use your imagination to try to make this dossier look like a secret file.

SECRET DOSSIER

NAME _____

AGE _____

APPEARANCE _____

BEHAVIOUR _____

FRIENDS _____

DANGER TO THE STATE _____

This will have to be a guess.

Look at what Caesar says in lines 191–209.

This scene gives you two names: add more later.

What does his conversation with Brutus show he is plotting? Look at lines 25–176 and his last speech in this scene, lines 308–322.

Persuasion   *lines 25–307*

A good deal of this scene is taken up with Cassius' attempt to persuade Brutus to join his party of conspirators. How would you set about persuading a friend to do something which you think is right but which he or she has doubts about?

 Imagine you are out shopping. You are trying to persuade your friend to buy a new pair of jeans which are a bargain – but your friend feels the money should really be saved for a special birthday present for their Mum. How would you set about the persuasion?

Work with a partner to try out such a conversation.

Now, still in the same pairs, take a look at what Cassius says to influence Brutus.

Look at his speeches to Brutus in three sections:

1   lines 55–78: he says here he is able to show Brutus his own inner self just as a mirror reflects his outward appearance. Between you, decide on one short quotation which seems to sum this up.

2   lines 90–131: here he tells his stories to prove that Caesar is an ordinary man with human weaknesses. Again, find your quotation to sum it up.

3   lines 134–160: what do you think he is suggesting here? Try to work out what his main point is and choose your key line or lines.

Brutus listens carefully to Casca's account of Caesar's being offered the crown. If Caesar really wanted to accept it, as Casca thinks, then this brings nearer what Brutus fears – rule by Caesar alone and by his heirs after his death. Pick another key line or two from this section (lines 214–306) to add to your selection.

Write your quotations out and compare your choice with the lines the rest of the class has chosen.

Brutus   *lines 79–176*

Brutus does at least listen to the idea that Caesar must be stopped, but what is his reaction to Cassius? Discuss with a partner what success you feel Cassius' persuasions have had, and see if you can find any lines which offer evidence. Set up a class discussion on Brutus and contribute your ideas and the evidence you have found.

Casca   *lines 214–294*

Brutus says about Casca, a little later in this scene, 'What a blunt fellow is this grown to be!' Judging from Casca's account of the offer of the crown, what could Brutus mean by 'blunt', do you think? Does he sound the sort of man whom you could believe?

With your partner, look carefully at Casca's words, and try to work out what kind of person he is. From what Casca says, work out what he thinks of the offer of a crown to Caesar. Find some lines from his speeches which give clues to his thoughts and his feelings.

Compare your choice of lines with the rest of the class.

Cassius' schemes *lines 308–322*

When everyone has left, Cassius speaks his real thoughts to the audience in a soliloquy. This is a speech in which a character, alone on the stage, speaks directly to the audience. It's a useful way to see right into their secret feelings.

Read this speech through in pairs, taking alternate 'sense units' (usually marked off by full stops or semicolons). Then discuss with your partner what Cassius really thinks of Brutus and what his next plan is.

Cassius' letter

Make your own version of one of the letters Cassius intends to throw in at Brutus' window. The letter which Brutus discovers later on says: 'Brutus, thou sleep'st: awake and see thyself. Shall Rome, etc. Speak, strike, redress!'

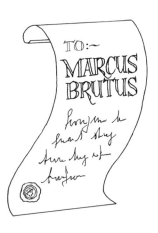

As you can see, this letter does not say anything too openly. ('Shall Rome, etc.' hides a lot of hints. It shows that Brutus is skimming over the words, leaving the audience to guess what they are.) It would be too dangerous to write down detailed suggestions about assassination or violence. So keep this in mind when you make up your letter; hint rather than tell him outright. Don't try to use Shakespeare's kind of language; just put it into your own words. You can then make a copy on 'parchment' by yellowing the paper with colour or scorching, and use an ancient kind of script to make it seem 'authentic'.

Display the letters on the wall for everyone to see.

A final thought on this scene

Who seems to you to be the leader of the conspiracy at this point? Discuss with your partner how you think things will develop. Note down your ideas.

Act 1 scene 3

14 March, late evening. A street in Rome.
There is a terrible storm raging in Rome and all sorts of strange events seem to have been happening, but Cassius is quite unmoved. He meets Casca, who is frightened by the storm, and persuades him to join the conspiracy. They go together to Brutus' house.

 ## Sound effects   *lines 3–13*

On the stage, a lot of the drama of this scene depends on the 'stage effects' of the storm. There are devices like wind machines and thunder sheets which can be used in the theatre, but you can do quite a lot just with the human voice. Pick out one short section to try to create your own storm.

Work in groups of six, or as a whole class. Concentrate on Casca's speech (lines 3–13). Three of you, or three groups of about three each, are to read the lines. Divide them like this:

1   Are you not mov'd . . . O Cicero!
2   I have seen tempests . . . tempest dropping fire.
3   Either there is civil strife . . . send destruction.

The rest of you are to make the sounds of the thunderstorm. If you can borrow cymbals or drums that could help, but find ways of creating the impression without them. You will need to 'orchestrate' these noises so the sounds do not drown the words: decide when they are to be loudest and get the readers to pause at the right moments.

Think carefully about what effect you are trying to achieve: the storm frightens Casca so it will need to seem sinister and frightening, not just noisy! Think about how this can be created in your short extract.

Perhaps you could tape your efforts to play back and listen to critically. Compare your taped version with the versions produced by the rest of the class.

Staging the scene

Try your hand at stage design. Here is a possible stage plan for this scene:

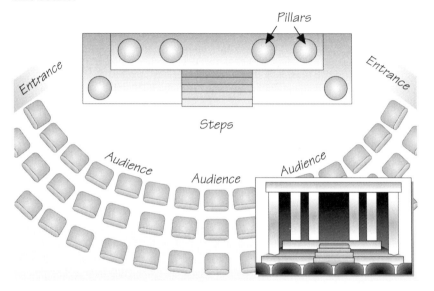

Work in threes. After all your work on the sound effects, you are going to think now about what the scene could *look* like. Either use the given stage plan or make one entirely of your own. Pick one point in the scene and write the line that is being spoken at that point underneath your plan. Then mark where each actor will be at that point in the scene: where the actors are going to enter and leave, and where they will stand on stage. Mark the entrances of the characters on your plan by arrows from the entrance to where the actor is to stand.

 If you have the space, it always helps to 'walk through' these moves to see if they feel natural.

A good general rule is always to have a reason for any move, however small – here it could well be to get closer in order to be heard above the storm, or because what is being said might be dangerous if it is overheard.

When you have finished planning the actors' moves, do these tasks between you:

- make a fair copy of the plan
- sketch the views the audience would have of the scene
- make notes for sound effects and lighting at the moment your chosen line is being spoken.

The stage plan provided is only a guide; you may wish to make yours a modern-dress production and that might well involve a very different setting.

When you've finished, act out your line according to your plan, and then display your work with everyone else's. Discuss what problems came up while you planned it.

Key to Cassius

The way Cassius reacts to the events of this stormy night gives us some useful clues to his character.

Working with a partner, compare the way he and Casca feel about the strange events of this night.

1   Which are the odd happenings that Casca finds so frightening? Look at lines 15–32 and make a list of them.

2   The Romans thought that unnatural events and great storms foretold the downfall of great men, but Cassius shows no sign of being superstitious. Perhaps he sees the storm as a symbol of Caesar's growing power and arrogance which he hopes will be stopped very soon. Cassius calls it 'a very pleasing night to honest men' (line 43) and says he feels no need to shelter from the weather. He seems to welcome the storm. Discuss why you think he says this.

3   The storm gives Cassius an excuse to start talking with Casca about Caesar and their plans, and to persuade him to join the conspirators. Find a line between 116 and 130 which shows that Casca has been won over, and add this to your notes.

4   Finally, choose two lines or phrases spoken by Cassius during this scene that seem to you to show his character most clearly. Write them down.

Act 2 scene 1

14 March, later that night. Brutus' orchard.
Brutus is worrying about the plan to assassinate Caesar. He counts himself a friend of Caesar, yet he fears that Caesar intends to become a king and take away the freedom of the Romans. When Cassius arrives with a group of conspirators, Brutus finally tells them that he has agreed to join them. They discuss their plans for the next day's move against Caesar. After they have all left, Brutus' wife, Portia, begs him to share his problems with her and he promises he will.

Brutus' thoughts   *lines 10–34*

The soliloquy of Brutus that begins the scene shows just how hard he finds it to decide to attack Caesar. He still keeps remembering he is Caesar's friend, yet he knows he must do what he can to prevent a dictatorship.

Start by tracing the thread of Brutus' arguments: find one line to sum up each of the following stages:

1   He has no personal quarrel with Caesar.
2   He fears that being king would change Caesar.
3   Ambition may begin in a humble nature, but once greatness is achieved, that nature will forget its humble beginnings.
4   Caesar will have to be killed not for what he is, but for what he might become.

Images

Now think about the images Brutus uses to express his fears. His language in this speech is full of imaginative comparisons which create pictures of these thoughts and fears.

Images are examples of language used metaphorically, not literally or factually. For instance, when Brutus compares Caesar with a snake's egg which is harmless at present but could be very dangerous later, he is not speaking literally. Caesar and the egg are not alike in any factual sense. The comparison is just a good way for Brutus to think about the possibility of danger.

Image search

Find the following in lines 10–34:

1   Brutus sees Caesar as a .... (a dangerous creature that hides and suddenly strikes) in the danger he presents to Rome.
2   He tells us that Caesar's ambition is the .... that will take him up above ordinary men, looking down on them and despising them.
3   Caesar, he says, is like the .... of a reptile, harmless now but likely to hatch into a deadly creature.

 Divided mind

Before you move on from this important speech, try another way of bringing out the conflict in Brutus' mind.

Work in threes for this activity: two of you are the two halves of Brutus' mind, divided about what to do, and the third is Brutus himself, listening to the opposing points of view.

Divide Brutus' speech, lines 10–34, into the two sides of Brutus' argument: the side which says that Caesar is dangerous, and the side which says he is good. (Lines 10–12, 19–21, and 28–30 will help you with this.)

Rehearse your version of this dialogue between the two halves of Brutus' mind and then 'perform' it, with the third person (representing Brutus) standing between the two halves of Brutus' mind. As each half speaks, Brutus turns to face it.

This third person is then asked what they felt was the stronger argument and also whether Brutus has really made up his mind about what to do by the end of this soliloquy.

All the Brutus characters should then report back to the rest of the class, saying which half of Brutus' mind had the most impact on them, and why.

Decision-making   *lines 86–228*

There are three important matters to be decided by the conspirators in this scene and Brutus and Cassius disagree about each of them. Find them, then copy and complete this chart.

DECISION 1	About the oath Lines 113–140	Whose advice is taken? Tick one.
Cassius thinks		
Brutus thinks		
DECISION 2	About Cicero being asked to join Lines 141–153	
Cassius thinks		
Brutus thinks		
DECISION 3	What should happen to Antony? Lines 155–183	
Cassius thinks		
Brutus thinks		

Portia   *lines 234–309*

The last part of this scene shows Brutus with his wife Portia, who demands to share in all his troubles. She has very few lines in the whole play but historically she was a remarkable woman.

Her conversation here with Brutus shows what kind of a man he is in his private life; their relationship rests on trust and sharing. Later you will find a contrast with the marriage of Calphurnia and Caesar. (See also the section on the women in the play, page 72.)

With your partner, read Portia's conversation with Brutus (lines 234–309) and make your own notes on the following points:

- What kind of things has she noticed out of the ordinary in Brutus' behaviour recently?
- How does she dismiss his feeble excuse?
- What right does she say she has to share the troubles of his mind?
- She claims to be more than just an ordinary woman. Who was her father?

Brutus' reactions

Find a line or phrase that proves each of these statements:

- Brutus truly loves his wife.
- He does not think he deserves such a noble wife.
- He is convinced by her arguments and agrees to tell her everything.

Stage directions

Modern dramatists show how they want a character to behave by using *stage directions*: sometimes they even describe the character for the reader of the play to picture. Shakespeare hardly ever gives any stage directions and most of the ones in the copies of the play you have were added by editors. But sometimes what the characters should be doing or how they should be moving is obvious from what is said.

You are going to fill out the details about Portia by inventing the stage directions for a short extract from one of her speeches.

Work with a partner and choose a section of about ten lines and either photocopy or write out the lines in the middle of a large sheet of paper, leaving plenty of space round the outside.

Decide how those lines are to be spoken, and any moves Portia is to make during them. Write in on one side, next to the appropriate lines, your chosen moves – like 'Move closer to Brutus' or 'Turn away to right/left'. On the other side add your ideas of *how* she should say the lines – for example 'quickly', 'urgently'. Try out the lines if it helps you.

Add a few more directions, too: at the beginning, put a description of what kind of a person she is, and put in directions for the music or stage lighting you may wish to use.

 Now get another pair to try out your speech, using your stage directions, and you try out theirs, so you can tell whether your versions work dramatically.

Ligarius   *lines 310–334*

Work with a partner. Look at the way this scene ends. Ligarius is a sick man, yet he is ready to throw off his illness to join the conspirators.

Discuss and note down your ideas about:
- why Shakespeare includes Ligarius at the end of the scene
- what makes Ligarius suddenly well again
- what shows the importance of Brutus to the assassination plot.

Act 2 scene 2

15 March (the Ides of March), morning. Caesar's house. Caesar's wife, Calphurnia, is worried about the bad omens of this past night, and the ominous dreams she has had. She tries to stop Caesar going to the Capitol, but when some of the conspirators arrive to escort him there, he is soon persuaded to go with them.

Omens and predictions   *lines 1–37*

Work with a partner to make up the front page of a tabloid newspaper, describing some of the strange events of the night of 14 March. You will find some mentioned here but there are others in Act 1 scene 3, described by Casca. Choose one or two that seem to offer the best front page headlines and write up the reports, sharing the work between you.

If you have time, add a horoscope expert commenting on the meaning of the events on an inside page. You will probably have seen articles like this in modern newspapers, where a fortune teller (usually called 'Gypsy Meg', or something like that) examines the omens for the Royal Family or the Prime Minister in the coming year.

ONLY / **THE DAILY** / **XIIp / ORATOR**

MAN'S HAND ON FIRE - REPORTS OF WONDERS FLOOD IN...

March XV   Today's Gladiators: Pages XX–XXI

INSIDE: Accident or omens?
GYPSY PEDRO COMMENTS

Exclusive oracles in **YOUR DAILY ORATOR**

STORM
OF THE
CENTURY!

LION SEEN IN CAPITOL
Eyewitness report • Page III

Caesar's horoscope   *lines 38–107*

These omens are not the only signs that something terrible is going to happen. When the priests, on Caesar's orders, kill the animal sacrifice and cut it open, they find no heart (line 40).

To the Romans this would seem a sign that some dreadful disaster is about to happen. No wonder Calphurnia is alarmed by this, as well as by her dreams.

What are these dreams that have disturbed her so much (line 3 and lines 76–81)? What does Calphurnia fear the omens and the dreams foretell?

Caesar answers some of her fears, by interpreting the animal sacrifice in a different way, and Decius has even more reassuring interpretations of her dreams.

Find out what each of them says and fill in their points, in your own words, on the chart below.

Animal sacrifice: what was found?	Sinister interpretation:	Reassuring interpretation (offered by Caesar, lines 41–43):
No heart in carcass		

Calphurnia's dream: what did she dream of?	Sinister interpretation:	Reassuring interpretation (offered by Decius, lines 84–90):

Produce some drawings of the dreams, visions, and omens in lines 1–82 and make a display to put on the wall.

Now see if you can find another piece of information that Decius gives which may influence Caesar even more (lines 93–96).

So Caesar leaves for the Senate – and his death.

The whole scene is full of bad omens and fears, and the effect on the audience is to lead them to expect disaster. Remember too the warning of the Soothsayer in Act 1 scene 2 – 'Beware the Ides of March' – this very day, 15 March.

Now imagine that, in a modern setting, these warnings are included in a horoscope for Caesar, to appear in a magazine. These horoscopes always wrap the warnings up in some favourable forecasts and promises of good fortune – always very vague, of course. Try to do this with the warnings for Caesar. Hint at the promise of the crown perhaps, and at how popular and well-loved Caesar is.

To remind you of the sort of language these horoscopes use, here is an example:

Pisces: *Feb. 19–Mar. 18*
Another one of those confusing months when you don't quite know where you stand; this could be an unsettling month for you. Planetary action is likely to affect your life. The position of Mars suggests this could be a good time to embark on a new enterprise but it could also spell trouble for your domestic life. News may arrive of a long-lost friend but you should beware of rushing into any new relationship.

(Notice the vagueness of 'should beware', 'suggests', and 'could be', and the mixture of promise and warning!)

Calphurnia's diary

In the end no one listens to Calphurnia and she makes no further protest when Caesar decides to go to the Capitol. But do you think she is really reassured by what Decius has said?

Either imagine she is recording her feelings in her diary, just after the others have left. Make up her entry for the morning of 15 March.

Or choose someone to be Calphurnia and get her to answer questions from the rest of the class about what she feels at this time. Then discuss whether you agree with her replies.

Act 2 scenes 3 and 4

15 March, a little later the same day. Artemidorus has found out something about the assassination attempt and he plans to warn Caesar. Portia's anxiety shows that Brutus has kept his word and confided in her; she is very much afraid things will go wrong with their plans.

Scene 3: the conspirators' defence *lines 1–14*

If Caesar had read this warning of Artemidorus in time, he might have been able to save himself. The conspirators would probably have been arrested and brought to trial.

Choose one of the conspirators we know very little about – Metellus Cimber perhaps, or Cinna.

He is to be defended by his defence counsel, who is trying to prove him innocent.

In pairs, make up all the arguments this conspirator could use in his defence. Here are some suggestions to help you:

- his love of Rome
- Caesar was becoming too powerful
- he was misled by Cassius.

He will be questioned by the prosecution, which is trying to prove him guilty.

In the same pairs, make up the questions to be put by the prosecution.

Then as a class, stage a trial, with pairs taking it in turns to be conspirator and defence counsel, and the rest of the class as the prosecution. Try to come to a fair verdict!

Scene 4: Portia's thoughts

Portia is in a state of near panic as she listens for any sound that may offer a clue as to what is happening (line 18). Then she hears from the Soothsayer that he intends to warn Caesar again, which makes her even more disturbed.

Write down her thoughts as she waits for news. Write them in a stream without proper sentences or full stops so that you show her troubled and confused state of mind. Dashes are useful, too – and disjointed scraps of phrases. This will give the impression that she is very disturbed and worried, and can't quite think straight. Compare your work with others in the class.

Act 3 scene 1

15 March (the Ides of March). The Capitol. ★
Caesar does not listen to the warnings, and the conspirators
manage to get close to him. They all stab him and he falls dead.
Antony has fled to his house on hearing the news, but the
conspirators agree to his request to speak with them and he
shakes each of them by the hand. Although Cassius warns
against it, Brutus gives permission for Antony to speak at
Caesar's funeral, after he, Brutus, has given their reasons for the
assassination. When the others leave, Antony's real feelings and
his desire for revenge become clear.

The assassination

Turn back to the bit of this scene which shows the actual
stabbing of Caesar (lines 58–84) and have another close look at
it, reading silently.

What do you think is in each of the conspirators' minds at the
moment of the assassination? What reasons and motives have
brought them to this point? What do they think of Caesar as they
stab him? What does Caesar feel in his last moments?

Copy and complete the chart below on how Caesar felt as he was
attacked.

What does Caesar feel about the attack?	Amazed. Thought he was well loved.
Is he surprised that Brutus is one of the attackers?	
Is he surprised that Cassius is involved?	No. He knew he was dangerous.
What was his opinion of himself? (Look at lines 58–73)	

★The Capitol was one of the seven hills of Rome, and the Forum – the
administrative centre of Rome – was at its foot.

We have very little information about many of the conspirators in this scene, but we have learnt more about a few of them – Cassius, Brutus, Casca, and Decius – so these are the ones to concentrate on.

The chart below tries to show the view each of the conspirators took of Caesar and to suggest likely motives for their actions. See if you agree with the parts already filled in and then try to fill in the rest for yourself. You may have to base some of your answers on your opinion of the characters, rather than on what they actually say in the play.

CHARACTER	VIEW OF CAESAR	MOTIVE FOR ASSASSINATION
Cassius	A man, not a god. Wants to be king.	
Brutus		To help Rome remain free.
Casca		
Decius	Easily influenced.	

Write your own soliloquy

Divide into groups of five. Each person chooses to be one of the characters on the charts – Caesar, or one of the conspirators.

In turn, tell the rest of the group what you think your character feels, and (if you are one of the conspirators) why you find yourself there with a dagger in your hand. The character descriptions on pages 67–68 may help you.

When you have each had a turn at this, go away by yourself to write an extra speech – your character's soliloquy about your feelings as you stab Caesar, or, in the case of Caesar himself, what you are thinking about the treachery of these men who are killing you.

Now come back together, read and act the lines from 31 to the Casca's line 'Speak, hands, for me!', then freeze the action. Each in turn steps out of the freeze frame to speak his soliloquy directly to the audience. Then go back to the action and finish stabbing Caesar. You may need to practice this several times.

Share your scene with the rest of the class and discuss the effect.

Your judgement about Caesar

This is a good place to pause and think about Caesar's character and what he thought about others as well as what they thought about him.

Look at this spider graph, showing what he thought of some of them.

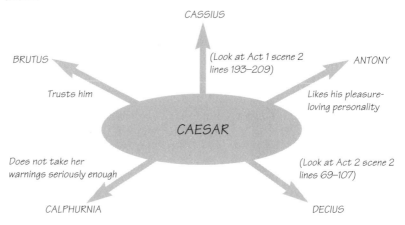

CASSIUS

BRUTUS

(Look at Act 1 scene 2 lines 193–209)

ANTONY

Trusts him

Likes his pleasure-loving personality

CAESAR

Does not take her warnings seriously enough

(Look at Act 2 scene 2 lines 69–107)

CALPHURNIA

DECIUS

Copy it and complete it for yourself; compare notes with a partner.

Copy the names again on a new diagram but turn the arrows the other way, and use this second spider graph to show what others thought of Caesar. (This time you could add Casca.)

Production of the assassination   *lines 58–84*

Did you find the actual stabbing of Caesar tended to produce some unwanted laughs? It is always difficult to present violence on the stage without going 'over the top' and tipping the scene into comedy, especially when you have had little chance to create the right atmosphere beforehand.

Work in groups of five or six to try out different ways of presenting Caesar's death. First, try making the stabbings symbolic only, with daggers brought down on Caesar in slow motion. (You may have seen this technique used in films and on television at moments of violence: the action slows down dramatically, as if that is how the person involved might see the event.)

Then try a more savage attack – apparently more realistic, but of course only creating the illusion of violence. (Actors have to learn many techniques to *appear* to be violent, but never hurt each other.)

Pause here to discuss which of these approaches would work best for the audience. Which of them would make the audience sympathetic to the conspirators? Which would make Caesar seem more of a victim?

You will see that a director's overall interpretation of the play will make a difference to the way the assassination is to be played.

 ## The conspirators attack

There is another director's decision to be made about this scene. We know that Casca strikes first and that Brutus is last but there are no indications about the order in which the others stab. We just know that they had decided that everyone must join in, so they would all share the responsibility afterwards.

Discuss as a class what order would work best and then choose enough actors to try it out. The rest of you are the audience and should comment afterwards on how well it worked.

Your opinions

Set up a class discussion on these two questions:
1 Did Caesar really intend to become King?
2 Was there no way to stop him except by murder?

Prepare for your discussion by looking at the evidence:

For 1:
- He wants Calphurnia to bear a child (a king would pass on the crown to his heirs), Act 1 scene 2
- He seems to be influenced by Decius' comments about the Senate's intention to offer him a crown when he is hesitating about going to the Capitol, Act 2 scene 2
- Casca's account of what happens offstage in Act 1 scene 2 lines 233–287
- Caesar's view of himself in Act 1 scene 2 lines 35–73.

For 2:
No one in the play suggests an alternative way of curbing Caesar's power, other than killing him. Was there a choice? Work out your ideas in pairs before the class discussion.

In your discussion remember there are no 'right' answers: you can have any opinions about them, as long as you can point to reasons for them.

Antony's reactions   *lines 147–297*

It isn't until his soliloquy (lines 254–275) that we realize just how hard it has been for Antony to pretend to be friendly with the men who have killed Caesar. But when you then think back over the scene you realize there were some clues. Look at his very first speech here, 'O mighty Caesar, dost thou lie so low?' (lines 148–163), when he asks that he may die here and now beside his friend. After the reassurances he receives from Brutus and Cassius, when he shakes the hands of all the conspirators in turn, he almost gets carried away by his sorrow (lines 194–210). Then he asks permission to speak in Caesar's funeral, which Brutus gives, despite Cassius' warnings.

Work with a partner. Look back over these speeches and agree on two short extracts (both taken from *before* the soliloquy, which begins on line 254):

- one which you feel shows Antony's true feelings most clearly
- one which shows where he is most obviously pretending friendship towards the conspirators.

Copy the drawing of Antony and write the chosen bits in the two bubbles – the 'speaks' one and the 'thinks' one.

Antony's soliloquy

lines 254–275

Read the speech through with your partner, taking alternate 'sense units' (usually marked off by full stops or semicolons).

You are both part of Antony's thoughts; try to put expression into the lines as if he is thinking through the situation he finds himself in and releasing all the pent-up feelings he could not show when the conspirators were there.

Image search

Antony's strong feelings of grief and his desire for revenge show in his images of Caesar's dead body and the consequences of the murder.

You will each need a copy of Antony's soliloquy (lines 254–275), written out or photocopied, stuck in the middle of a large sheet.

Still in your pairs, find and underline on your sheet the lines that show the following:

1   A picture of Caesar's wounds wanting to speak to us and tell of his murder.
2   A picture of a world where violence will become so common that mothers will feel nothing when their children are slaughtered.
3   The goddess of Revenge let loose from Hell.
4   War seen as fierce dogs let off the lead for attack.
5   The evil of Caesar's murder as a smell of rotting flesh.

Next, working on your own, use the space all round the speech to add your own comments about Antony's feelings, what he intends to do, and details of his language, linking all your points by arrows to the line they connect with most closely. Just add anything that strikes you about the speech or any part of it. Compare your work with your partner's, and pool your ideas; keep this piece of work to use later when looking at the character of Antony.

Here is an example of the kind of things you might write:

Speaks directly to the body   *Blood – emotional*

O pardon me <u>thou</u> <u>bleeding</u> piece of earth,
That I am meek and gentle with these <u>butchers</u>.
Thou art the ruins of the <u>noblest man</u>   *Makes conspirators*
<u>That ever lived</u> in the tide of times.   *seem heartless brutes*
Shows his hero-worship of Caesar

Act 3 scene 2

15 March, later that day. The Forum. *
Brutus and Antony address the Roman citizens. After Brutus' speech they seem to be convinced by his arguments, but Antony's funeral speech for Caesar very cleverly sways them to feel sorry for Caesar and angry with the conspirators for killing him. They are ready to seek revenge for Caesar's murder. At the end of the scene, news comes of the arrival of Caesar's nephew, Octavius, in Rome, and of the flight of Cassius and Brutus from Rome.

*The Forum was the administrative centre of Rome – the centre of government. It contained a platform from which the citizens could be addressed.

Techniques of persuasion: Brutus   *lines 1–63*

Look at Brutus' speech to the citizens first. He speaks very simply and straightforwardly of his reasons for killing Caesar. Using these notes, try to write down a summary of his defence of his action.

1   He loved Caesar but .... (line 23).
2   He feared that Caesar intended to make Romans .... (line 24).
3   He mourns Caesar's death and honours his past bravery but his .... made it necessary to kill him (line 30).
4   He is ready to .... himself if Rome asks it of him (line 48).

Notice that Shakespeare gives an early hint that Brutus may not have been as successful as he at first seems, because one of the crowd calls out that *Brutus* should become Caesar (line 52). Someone, at any rate, has not quite got the message!

Antony's speeches to the citizens   *lines 75–253*

Antony's speeches are far more subtle than Brutus', and are full of very clever ways of manipulating his audience – working at times in the same way as modern politicians do to influence people to vote for them.

The illustration opposite shows six of the clever tricks Antony uses. Working with a partner, find some of the other tricks in his speech. Work out a way to label the trick, as in the illustration, and write down the line numbers. Some ideas to look for:

- what he says about Brutus
- what he means when he uses the word 'honourable'
- how he flatters the citizens
- what he says of Caesar's victory in battle
- how he talks of blood, to move the citizens to pity and anger
- how he uses the body of Caesar to move the citizens.

There are still more to be found!

Make your own new illustration, writing in your labels and line numbers.

REPETITION

Which phrases are repeated? and with what effect?

RHETORICAL QUESTIONS
asked for dramatic effect – do not require an answer.
(e.g. lines 92, 99, 105)

PRETENCE THAT HE IS NO GOOD AT PUBLIC SPEAKING
(see lines 217–223)

EXAMPLES of Caesar's noble and generous behaviour.
(e.g. lines 90 & 93)

CAESAR'S WILL
used as a stage prop.
(e.g. lines 130 & 239)

CAESAR'S CLOAK – pretends to know who made which wound.
(see lines 175–181)

Bare bones

Work in groups of six. Each person chooses one of Antony's tricks, either from the illustration, or from your own findings.

From Antony's speeches, choose the best lines to illustrate your chosen trick, and write them down. Now the whole group puts these examples together in any order (with a word or two to link them where necessary) to make up a short speech, which should contain all the 'bare bones' of Antony's arguments.

Present a performance of your group's speech to the rest of the class, with everyone in your group speaking at least one set of lines in it. Compare the lines you chose with those the other groups selected.

Antony uses some skilful tricks that you couldn't hope to include by your method – like the constant repetition of 'ambition' and 'honourable men'. A brief summary can only convey some of Antony's clever oratory, but perhaps your cut-down version helped you to see how the original is made up.

Discuss as a class what was missing from the class versions, compared with Antony's speeches.

The citizens

The citizens are at first reluctant to stay and listen to Antony; they only do so because Brutus asks them to. (Look at lines 55–73.) But they gradually change sides as Antony speaks. With the help of the following questions, see if you can trace the stages by which this happens.

1 Which is the first line from a citizen that shows that Antony's first long speech (lines 75–109) is having some effect?
2 Pick out one of the citizens' lines which shows that Antony's message about the accusation of 'ambition' in Caesar has got home to them.
3 How do they now feel about Antony himself? Find one line as evidence.
4 After the next section of his speech (lines 120–139) what is the reaction? Find one line as evidence.
5 What feelings do they now have about the conspirators (lines 155 and 157)?
6 How do they feel about Caesar when they see his body? Choose a line to sum it up.
7 Gradually, Antony turns their grief into desire for revenge. Which is the first line that shows this?
8 Find one or two lines from the citizens towards the end of the scene that show their intentions now. Note down the lines you find.

Acting the scene

After you have found your way through these stages in the reactions of the citizens, you are ready to perform this very dramatic scene for yourselves.

Choose someone to be Antony, or ask your teacher to read his part; all the rest of you are the citizens. Ignore the 'first' and 'second' labels and ask your teacher to allocate at least one citizen's line to each of you. When they are just labelled 'Citizens' everyone can join in.

Now try to learn your line and the cue for it so that you don't have to follow the scene in the book and can actually listen and react to what Antony says. Rehearse the scene, and as well as saying your own lines, try to react to Antony's words in the ways you noted down earlier about the citizens' reactions. You will also need to add some extra reactions from the crowd: for instance a murmur of sympathy when Antony says he is so overcome he will have to pause to recover before he can go on (line 108), and possibly a gasp when Caesar's body is displayed. Add any others you can think of, but don't make them too strong to begin with; you need to build up to a climax so you must keep something in reserve until you need it.

After your rehearsal, present your final performance – which can be either like a radio play (which you could tape) or like a stage performance with added actions if you have the space to do this. Present your version to another class, or play the tape back to listen to yourselves.

Act 3 scene 3

15 March, evening. A street in Rome.
Cinna the poet is attacked by a crowd, merely because he shares the name Cinna with one of the conspirators.

Violence grows! Cinna the poet

Get into groups of five or six to dramatize this scene. Cinna the poet is minding his own business when he is set upon by a crowd of thugs. Think of ways of building up the tension gradually: the questions could start quite mildly with the citizens a little way from Cinna; then they could move in closer and closer with each question, becoming more aggressive as they do so, until he is surrounded and perhaps pushed from one to another. Build up to the climax of the end – 'Tear him! Tear him!' – when they hide him from the audience and then move away, leaving him in a heap on the floor. (These are only suggestions – work out your own ideas of presenting the scene.)

Make it a rule that all 'violence' must be symbolically shown or in slow motion, with no actual bodily contact at all.

It is hard to do this scene – or any scene – with books in your hands, so you may prefer to put them down after a few runs-through and just remember the gist of what you say instead of the exact lines.

Crowd or mob?

Pause for a little while when you have presented this scene, and on your own think about why Shakespeare put the scene in. Perhaps he wanted to show that violence breeds more violence? That assassinating Caesar led directly to this mindless attack? Or was it Antony's speech that set off the violence in the citizens?

What differences do you notice between the behaviour of the crowd here and the holiday atmosphere of Act 1 scene 1, when they were celebrating Caesar's victory over Pompey? There are obvious differences – but what is there which is similar? Make some notes of your own in answer to all these questions. You will need them for a later activity.

Act 4 scene 1

Some time later. A room in Antony's house.
This is the equivalent of the violence of the previous scene – this time, govenment violence rather than private violence. The three who now rule Rome – Antony, Octavius, and Lepidus – are bargaining over who should be executed, in a cold-blooded way. They also wish to avoid paying out too much under Caesar's will. We see, too, that Antony despises Lepidus and does not wish to share power with such a man.

Passage of time

What do you think has happened between the end of the previous scene and this? We have very little information about the time that has passed, but it must be some time later. Power is clearly in the hands of the Caesar camp again (even though Caesar himself is dead), and the conspirators are dead or have fled.

Status struggle

It is clear from this scene that there are tensions amongst the Triumvirate (rule by three men) made up of Antony, Octavius, and Lepidus. Antony doesn't think much of Lepidus' ability to rule at all and says so to Octavius when Lepidus has been sent on an errand. Can you find at least one line that shows this? Write it down in your notes.

There are also some hints that Antony and Octavius are not entirely in agreement. Find one example of this, too, and note it down.

The scene seems to be full of people giving one another instructions to do something or other.

See if you can find the following:

■ Antony sends Lepidus off to .... (line 7).
■ He tells Octavius not to speak of Lepidus with ....
(line 39).
■ Octavius tells Antony to mark someone down to ..... (line 3).

It seems that both Antony and Octavius want to be giving the orders in the new regine.

Do you think there is a parallel between Caesar and Antony? Does Antony now want to increase his personal power just as Caesar seemed to? Is that why he wants to assert himself in his contacts with Octavius? Note down your ideas on these questions so far.

Work in groups of three to make up a freeze frame which shows in some way the struggle to be boss in this Triumvirate. Lepidus would perhaps be below the other two and they would be trying to be top dog. Antony might be gesturing to Lepidus to go on an errand and Octavius ticking off names of those who are to die in their 'purge'. Show your freeze frame to the rest of the class and explain briefly what you wanted to show.

Act 4 scenes 2 and 3

Some weeks later. The rebel camp at Sardis.
Cassius and Brutus quarrel about Cassius' defence of a man condemned for taking bribes. The unusual anger of Brutus is explained by the news that his wife, Portia, has committed suicide. He and Cassius make up the quarrel and plan the battle to come. After he is left alone, Brutus sees the ghost of Julius Caesar who promises to see him the next day at the battle, at Philippi.

Scene 2: the quarrel begins   *lines 42–45*

Brutus is anxious they should not quarrel in front of their men. Why should this be so important? Note down your answer.

Soldiers

Working in pairs, pretend you are soldiers in Brutus' army and have noticed Cassius' loud and angry words (line 37). Make up a short conversation about it, in which you also mention the rumours that have been circulating about their disagreement. You might have heard that Brutus is angry with Cassius for supporting someone who has been taking bribes. Whose side would you be on? Do you think Brutus would have the respect of his men? See if you can show in your bit of dialogue what his soldiers think of him.

When you have worked out your conversation, show your ideas to another pair and listen to theirs.

Scene 3: film script   *lines 1–115*

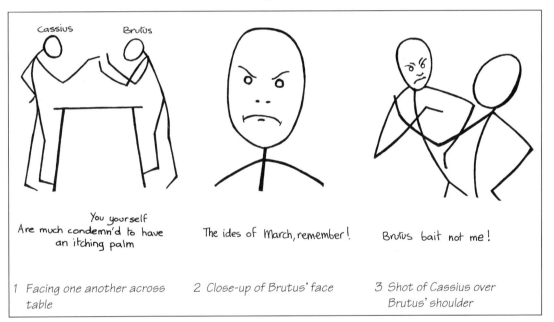

Cassius Brutus		
You yourself Are much condemn'd to have an itching palm	The ides of March, remember!	Brutus bait not me!
1 Facing one another across table	2 Close-up of Brutus' face	3 Shot of Cassius over Brutus' shoulder

Working on your own, imagine you are making a film of this quarrel between Cassius and Brutus. Look through it again and decide on a short section of about twenty-five to thirty lines as a sample. You will need to choose what camera shots will bring out most effectively the conflict between them in your chosen passage and to draw up a storyboard to show them.

You don't need technical terms, except perhaps 'close-up' and 'wide-angle', as your storyboard should show the way the camera will film the characters and the scene. Each time you want to change to a different shot, write the line of dialogue underneath and sketch, with stick people, what the camera will film. Your sketch could also show how you want your actors to stand, move, and gesture.

 It might help to get two other people to read your section of script for you so you can watch them and decide on your shots without having to look at the book at the same time. You can do the same for them.

If you have the equipment and the time, use a video camera to record your section and show it to the rest of the class.

Making up the quarrel   *lines 92–161*

Cassius seems very hurt at the rejection he feels from his friend Brutus and what he sees as the refusal to forgive his faults (line 89). He does admit his temper is quick, inherited from his mother (line 119), and Brutus, too, is ready to apologize (line 115). So the quarrel is made up with a handshake before the Poet breaks in to reproach them and the tension is broken with their laughter (line 132). When Cassius realizes that Portia has killed herself, he is even more sorry for his anger (lines 146–150).

Work with a partner. Have you ever quarrelled with a close friend? Most people find that being friends with someone doesn't mean you never disagree or don't get angry at times. What do you think is the effect of this quarrel between Cassius and Brutus? Does their friendship suffer as a result? Discuss these points with your partner and remember it is a matter of opinion, not of right or wrong answers. Finally, write down two quotations from the scene – one from Brutus to show the real feelings he has for Cassius, and one from Cassius to show how he feels about his friend, Brutus.

Portia's death: director's decision   *lines 162–194*

Work in the same pairs. There seems to be a muddle in the copy of the play that we have: Messala breaks the news of Portia's death after we have already heard it from Brutus himself. There is no way of knowing which was the original intention, but it is very unlikely we were meant to hear the news twice like this. If you were directing the play, which bit would you cut, and why? Discuss this with your partner, and write down your decision and your reason.

The Ghost on film   *lines 262–306*

At the end of the scene, Brutus sees the Ghost of Caesar. How could you handle this on film? What sound effects would you use? What lighting? What could the Ghost itself look like? Would it be transparent or covered in blood?

Work with a partner or on your own. Work out how you would have the Ghost appear and disappear, move and speak. Produce three sketches or storyboards to show the ghost appearing, speaking to Brutus, and disappearing in your version.

The Ghost in the theatre

There are fewer technical tricks available to a stage director than to a film director. How can you make the actor playing Caesar look like a ghost? Think about the make-up, sound and lighting effects you could use to create the right atmosphere.

Write your director's notes for your stage manager and the make-up person. (The job of a stage manager is to organize all the backstage crew, including lighting and sound experts and musicians; he or she also has to 'cue them in' at the right moments.)

The effect of the Ghost

What do you feel is the effect on the audience of the Ghost's appearance? What does it make you feel about Brutus' chances at Philippi? How does Brutus feel about it, do you think? Look at line 284.

Write down some rough notes of your opinions, to be used later when another appearance of the Ghost is mentioned.

Act 5 scene 1

The same day, at Philippi.
Antony and Octavius argue about their battle positions. They
exchange insults with Brutus and Cassius.

Power struggle – Antony and Octavius   *lines 1–20*

Antony and Octavius disagree again (do you remember what
they disagreed about in Act 4 scene 1?) – this time about who
should take the right hand side in the battle formation. This
might seem very trival, but it was traditional for the commander-
in-chief of a Roman army to take this position, so the
disagreement is all about status once more. Who do you think
wins this round? There's no stage direction to tell us who
actually takes up the right side.

 ### Words before blows   *lines 21–66*

Divide the whole class into two halves – one for each of the
opposing armies. Now look through the lines they shout at each
other and pick one from your side's lines as your chosen insult.

Form up in two lines facing one another and each in turn shout
your chosen line at your opposite number in the opposing army.
Each army takes alternate turns. It doesn't matter if several
people choose the same line – just look your enemy in the eye
and deliver your line as insultingly as you can.

Farewells   *lines 92–125*

After this exchange of insults and challenges, Brutus and Cassius
say their farewells to each other in case either of them should fall
in the coming battle. Think about what might be going through
their minds as they leave one another, for what may be the last
time. Brutus may be remembering Caesar's ghost which
appeared to him in Act 4 scene 3 lines 274–284; Cassius may be
thinking what a mistake it was to listen to Brutus and let Antony
speak in Caesar's funeral. Perhaps both of them may be thinking
of all the high hopes they had for a better Rome.

Work in pairs and make up a stream of thoughts for each of them. You can write a script for them or you can just make notes and improvise. Present your speeches to the rest of the class and listen to theirs.

Antony analysis

We have learnt a lot about Antony since Caesar's death, and this is a good point to think back over the play so far and see what we have discovered about his character.

A good way to start is to look at what other people in the play think of him. Copy the diagram and complete the spaces left. You may have to look back over earlier bits of the play to find some of the information, as the notes round the outside show you.

There are a couple of points to add, from this present scene. Octavius shows us at the beginning of it that he is determined to dominate Antony, and in line 62 Cassius calls Antony 'a masker and a reveller'. Add these opinions, too.

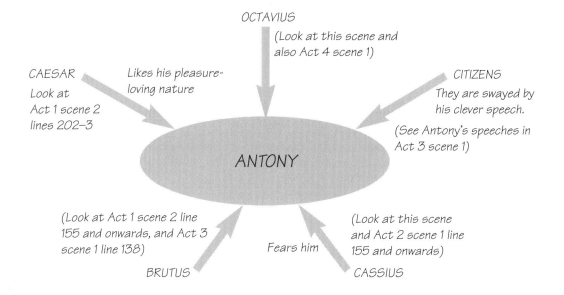

OCTAVIUS
(Look at this scene and also Act 4 scene 1)

CAESAR
Look at Act 1 scene 2 lines 202–3

Likes his pleasure-loving nature

CITIZENS
They are swayed by his clever speech.
(See Antony's speeches in Act 3 scene 1)

ANTONY

(Look at Act 1 scene 2 line 155 and onwards, and Act 3 scene 1 line 138)

Fears him

(Look at this scene and Act 2 scene 1 line 155 and onwards)

BRUTUS

CASSIUS

Act 5 scenes 2 and 3

Later the same day. The battlefield at Philippi.
Brutus feels the battle has started well, but Cassius' troops seem
to be surrounded. Cassius sends his friend, Titinius, to find out
what is going wrong and, through a misunderstanding, believes
it is his fault that Titinius is captured by the other side. He
orders his slave, Pindarus, to kill him. Titinius comes back with
their allies and finds Cassius is dead, so, when he is left alone,
he too chooses to die.

Scene 2: structure

This very short scene shows that Brutus is hopeful. Why do
you think it is separated from the next one and not part of the
same scene? Talk about it with a partner and then with your
teacher.

Scene 3: stages

This scene is very complicated and it is worth trying to divide it
up into several stages. See if you can complete these summaries
of each section.

1   lines 1–19: Cassius hears that Antony has captured his camp
    and sends to find out more.
2   lines 20–32: Pindarus reports what he thinks he sees:
    ....
3   lines 33–50: Cassius believes he has sent his friend to certain
    capture so he ....
4   lines 51–78: Titinius returns with Messala and finds
    ....
5   lines 79–90: he shows his loyalty and friendship to Cassius
    by ....
6   lines 91–110: Brutus enters and finds ....

Roman honour

It was an important part of the Roman code that you chose to
die rather than suffer the shame of being captured. Sometimes
you ran on your own sword, but this was very hard to do

effectively, so often you persuaded your servant or friend to kill you or to hold the sword for you to run on.

 ## Tell the story

Work in groups of three or four and choose four key moments from the scene which you can present as freeze frames to tell the story. If you haven't the space to present these, you could draw four pictures of these key moments, with stick people if you like, and write one line from the scene underneath each.

Audience sympathy

What do you think the audience feels about Cassius' death?

Think about how he dies: he commits suicide nobly, because he believes he has sent his friend to his capture and cannot face the feeling of guilt. Titinius' decision to die with Cassius shows that he inspires friendship of a very special kind.

Up to now he has been presented as a cunning manipulator (winning Brutus to his side by underhand means) and a man who defended a taker of bribes (in the quarrel with Brutus in Act 4 scene 3). Yet now he appears as a man with a real sense of honour and a very good friend.

Discuss these points with the class.

Weighing up Cassius

Divide the class into two: one half is to find all the admirable things about Cassius, and the other to look for evidence of his faults, each half finding lines which show these aspects of his character.

Use a really large sheet of paper to put on the wall with a line down the centre. On the right of it, one half of the class writes the points *in favour*, with suitable short quotations; on the left, the other half writes the points *against* with suitable short quotations. (It could be easier to get individuals to write their quotes on separate small pieces of paper and give a couple of people on each side the job of sticking them on the large sheet.)

If you think there are some things which are neither good nor bad, keep a space in the middle for these.

Below are some suggestions for how the work can be divided between groups:

In favour

1 The friendship with Titinius – see above. His bravery: Act 5 scene 3.
2 Cleverness – Caesar's comments: Act 1 scene 2 lines 200–202.
3 Recognizes Caesar's ambition: Act 1 scene 2 lines 134–149. Defence of Roman freedom.
4 Realism about danger that Antony poses: Act 2 scene 1 lines 155–161 and Act 3 scene 1 lines 232–243.
5 Friendship with Brutus and sympathy when Portia dies: Act 4 scene 3 line 149.

There are others for you to think of for yourselves.

Against

1 Underhand methods of persuasion of Brutus: Act 1 scene 2 lines 308–322.
2 Anger: quarrel with Brutus: Act 4 scenes 2 and 3.
3 Support for bribe-taker: Act 4 scene 3 lines 1–5.
4 Antony says he killed Caesar because he was envious: Act 5 scene 5 lines 69–70. Do you agree? If so, put it on the sheet.

Search for examples of all these and any others you can think of.

Act 5 scenes 4 and 5

The same day, still later. The battlefield at Philippi. Brutus' army fights bravely but is defeated, with Lucilius courageously pretending to be Brutus so as to give him time to get away. The remnants of his army are resting away from the battle and Brutus tries to persuade each of them in turn to kill him. Eventually one agrees and Brutus runs on to the sword he holds. Antony finds him dead and pays tribute to his noble nature.

Scene 4: battle scenes

In Shakespeare's day, battles were not presented realistically on the stage. A few actors marching on and off with a banner could easily represent a whole army. Modern audiences tend to expect less symbolic and more realistic action, especially in the cinema.

Discuss with a partner how you would stage a battle with no more than twenty actors in all, including the main characters in these scenes.

You might like to consider:
- how to show which side they are on
- how to give the impression of numbers
- how to give the impression of action and violence
- what to use to help give these impressions: clothes, music, noise.

When you have talked over the problems and possible solutions, try out the following idea.

 ### A battle in slow motion

Divide into groups of about five or six and read through the scene again from Cato's line: 'I will proclaim my name about the field' (line 3).

Now plan how you can stage the scene – but using your own words so you do not need books, and showing the fighting in slow motion. No one should touch anyone in these fights: stop just short of the other person with each blow or sword stroke.

This summary might help you when you come to make up your dialogue:
1　Cato dies at the hands of an enemy soldier.
2　Lucilius shouts that he is Marcus Brutus and is captured by enemy soldiers, who think they have taken Brutus himself.
3　Antony enters, is told of their great achievement and realizes it is not Brutus.
4　He hears Lucilius' reasons for the pretence and praises his bravery.

Scene 5: Brutus' request   *lines 1–51*

Unlike the last scene, there is no shouting in this scene – Brutus'
soldiers are exhausted (one falls asleep) and most of the dialogue
is in whispers. What is Brutus whispering to each of his men in
turn? In the end he gets Strato to agree to what he wants. What
is it? Discuss this with the whole class.

The Ghost of Caesar once again

In lines 17–19, Brutus tells Volumnius that Caesar's ghost has
appeared to him again. Look back to check what was said last
time – in Act 4 scene 3 line 274 – and imagine what the Ghost
might have said this time, here at Philippi before the battle.

 Work in pairs to make up this scene, between Brutus and
Caesar's Ghost, using your own words. What might the Ghost
say now? And what might Brutus reply?

Share your scene with another pair and watch theirs.

 ### Flashbacks

It is sometimes said that a drowning person sees the whole of
their life flash before their eyes at the moment of death. Imagine
that Brutus, dying on his own sword, can remember all the
events of his life that happen during this play. What would he
think of first? The first conversation with Cassius perhaps, that
put into words what he himself already feared? Here is a list of
what else he could have remembered:

■ his meeting with the conspirators at his own house
■ his conversation with Portia which followed
■ his part in the actual assassination
■ his speech to the citizens
■ his flight from Rome
■ the quarrel with Cassius, and the reconciliation
■ meeting Antony and Octavius before the battle
■ the final defeat at Philippi.

Work in small groups of four or five and choose any three of
these moments, or any others you like, which seem best to sum
up Brutus' part in this play, and make up a freeze frame to recall
each of them. Show them to the rest of the class and let them
guess which incidents you are showing. Alternatively, you could

draw pictures of these episodes and join them up to go round the walls as a frieze of Brutus' part in the play.

Headlines

This last scene of the play completes the action of the Battle of Philippi which started in scene 2. Look back over Act 5, scenes 2, 3, 4, and 5, and tell the story of them in a series of imaginary newspaper headlines, which trace the story of the battle from Brutus' hopeful start to his death. You can decide how many are needed.

This is the kind of headline to use:

THE ROMAN TIMES

TRAGIC MISTAKE SENDS CASSIUS TO DEATH

Add a few lines of writing under each, to expand the story a bit.

Display your headlines for everyone to see and discuss how successful they would be in telling the story to someone who had not read these last scenes.

Obituary

An obituary is a tribute to a dead person which appears in a newspaper and which concentrates on the person's good qualities and achievements during his or her life. It may refer to failures and even faults of character but the emphasis is always on the positive.

In a way, Antony's words about the dead Brutus are a sort of obituary, but they are very brief.

Write your obituary for Brutus, looking back over his life as you have seen it in the play, and paying tribute to his good qualities.

These are some of the things you might want to include:

- his friendship with Caesar
- motives in joining the conspirators
- respect of other Romans for him
- good relationship with wife and her tragic death recently.

The character profile of Brutus on page 67 may help you. What faults would you mention in passing? He wasn't a very good judge of character as far as Antony was concerned and he over-ruled Cassius on several points, unwisely. He was easy to persuade, wasn't he? Did this show he was gullible, do you think? (Look up this word in a dictionary if you need to.) Remember, Cassius said he wouldn't have been so easily persuaded if *he* had been Brutus.

You might begin rather like this:

OBITUARY

MARCUS BRUTUS

The life of one of the leaders of the conspiracy against Caesar finally ended yesterday. Marcus Brutus died on his own sword at the Battle of Philippi. He died, as he had lived – nobly . . .

Final thoughts

Think back over the last part of the play, since the death of Julius Caesar. It is strange that the person who gives his name to the whole play should die in Act 3 scene 1. But, even though he is dead, perhaps he doesn't disappear completely.

With a partner, remind yourselves of how Caesar lives on in the play after his assassination. Consider these questions:

- What does his Ghost say to Brutus on the eve of the battle of Philippi (Act 4 scene 3)?
- How does he live on in the play after that?
- How has he taken his revenge by the end? (Look at what Brutus says as he dies, Act 5 scene 5 lines 50–51.)

Note down your answers.

Consider, too, whom you feel most sorry for at the end.

Remember also what Antony prophesied after Brutus had agreed to his speaking at Caesar's funeral (Act 3 scene 1 lines 254–275). He swore that a curse should fall on those who did the deed, and that civil war and destruction would result. How has his prophecy come true?

Share your ideas with a partner and make some notes between you to prepare for a class discussion on the question, 'Nobody deserves to win in *Julius Caesar*'.

Overview

Characters

Character profiles

These character profiles describe the main characters as they are at a mid point in the play. They are intended to help you revise what you know of the characters after you have finished work on the play.

For a good revision exercise, complete these character profiles.

The profiles are also intended to give you a way in to the play, by providing information and background before you start reading.

Caesar

You are widely admired as a great man and hero. You are a brave and successful soldier and have just defeated Pompey in battle. You have a wife called Calphurnia, who, sad to say, cannot have children. This is important to you as you would like to be made king and have your children succeed you. But for the moment you are not ready to accept the offer of a crown; this would have to come from the Senate – the really important people in Rome. You are fond of your friend Antony who seems to get a good deal of fun out of life, but you know there are some dangerous plotters around you who need watching. You have the conviction that you are something special – not as other men – and are very proud. But you do have human frailties: you suffer from epilepsy, are rather deaf and by no means as tough as you would like to think.

Brutus

You count yourself as Caesar's friend, yet you are very disturbed at his growing ambitions, and you fear he may be made a king and so destroy the freedom of the Roman citizens. You are very trusting and always expect people to behave as nobly as you do yourself; this makes you a rather bad judge of character. You have a loving and noble wife, Portia, who shares in all you do and feel; you cannot bear to think of losing her. Like Caesar, you are an admired and successful soldier, highly respected by most Roman citizens.

Cassius

You are alarmed at Caesar's growing power and cannot see why he should be treated as a god on earth. You know he doesn't like you and you don't care for him. You are determined to oppose his ambition and the only way you can see of doing that is by assassinating him. You are good at persuading people to join your cause and not too fussy about the methods you use to do this, especially when you are after the support of such an important and respected ally as Brutus. You are a good judge of men and can usually see through to their real motives, because you don't have any illusions about them. You must have some noble qualities, however, as you inspire real loyalty, even to the point of death, in your friends.

Casca

You are a blunt, no-nonsense sort of person, but you know you don't like the way things are going in Rome, with Caesar growing so ambitious and powerful. You pride yourself on being a good judge of people and events and you're pretty sure Caesar really wants that crown. You're loyal to your friends and you don't tell tales!

Decius

You are very clever at reassuring people – that's why they get you to see that Caesar gets to the Senate on the fateful day. You really don't have a high opinion of a man like that who is so easy to convince.

Antony

You are a pleasure-loving person who enjoys plays and athletics, and you are close to Caesar, who trusts you. You are appalled at what happens to him and quite prepared to do whatever it takes to avenge his death. You are a very skilled public speaker and not always completely straightforward. You don't mind pretending and deceiving people if it will serve your purpose – and you do get things done. You don't care for the way your new ally, young Octavius, throws his weight about, but you need his assistance in defeating Brutus and Cassius.

Portia

You are the wife of Brutus and very loyal to him. You cannot bear to think he has worries and problems he has not been sharing with you. You know there is something on his mind and you must get to the bottom of it.

Calphurnia

You are Caesar's wife and naturally concerned about his safety and welfare, even though he sometimes seems to ignore you. You've been having worrying dreams recently which seem to be bad omens and these have alarmed you. You are used to being overruled by him but it doesn't stop you worrying.

Octavius Caesar

You return to Rome just at the moment of your uncle's death, to find that Antony has everything in hand and the conspirators already on the run. You see yourself, in many ways, as Julius Caesar's natural successor and you aren't going to be pushed around by anyone, even Antony.

These photos show Portia with Brutus (left), and Calphurnia with Caesar (above). What do you learn from them about the relationship each woman has with her husband?

Minor characters

The reasons for Shakespeare including these less important characters vary from one to another; some are needed to move the story on, some show us more about one of the major characters, some are used to increase the dramatic excitement (as when Artemidorus appears with a warning for Caesar and the audience doesn't know if he will get it to him in time or not).

Try to complete this chart of minor characters; some of the more difficult bits of it have been filled in for you.

	Moves plot on	Reveals other character	Contrast	Dramatic tension	Other reason	Further explanation
Lepidus			✓			Contrast with Antony and Octavius
Flavius and Marullus						
Ligarius		✓				Shows how great is Brutus' influence
Artemidorus						
Soothsayer						
Cinna the Poet						
Titinius		✓				Shows that Cassius inspires loyalty

Casting

How many actors would you need, to put on a performance of this play? In most real productions the director is restricted by costs to a limited number. Suppose you were doing a production of the play and you only had twenty-five actors. Could you make it work?

Work in pairs to draw up a list of all the characters and see what parts could be 'doubled up'. Remember you will need quite a few to make up the crowds which appear in Act 1 scene 1 and Act 3 scenes 2 and 3, and some to become soldiers in the various armies of Act 5. Actors who play named parts can also become members of the crowd at other times – make this clear on your list. For instance, Flavius and Marullus only appear in Act 1 scene 1; they could become conspirators by Act 2 scene 1 and then soldiers in Brutus' army in Act 5.

Make sure that if actors are playing more than one part, they will have time to change costume.

Compare notes with the rest of the class.

Statement game

Read through the following statements about some of the main characters in the play. They express very definite points of view and are open to question. How many of them do you agree with, on first reading?

1   Caesar is intent on one thing – to become king of Rome – but he wants it to be offered by the Senate, not the common people.

2   Cassius shows by his underhand tricks and interest in bribes that he would not have been fit to be one of Rome's rulers if the conspirators had succeeded.

3   Caesar treats Calphurnia like a piece of property and ignores her advice when it suits him.

4   Brutus' big mistake is to assume that everyone in the world is as high-minded as he is; this makes him behave very stupidly sometimes.

5   Brutus is bossy, too, and never listens to what others say, even when they understand people a great deal better than he does.

6   Antony is one of those people who believes the end justifies the means: he's quite prepared to use dishonest means if he thinks his cause is right – just like Cassius.

7   Antony shows his true colours when he himself becomes one of the three rulers – he is ambitious for power and ruthless in pursuing it.

8   The conspirators fail because they are not clever enough to see through Antony's schemes and because they are content to be constantly overruled by Brutus.

9 The citizens provide a strong argument against democracy; they aren't fit to decide anything because they are so easily led.

10 Portia is quite unnecessary to the play – she doesn't change anything and shows us nothing of Brutus we couldn't find out another way.

Divide into ten groups and allocate to each group one of the statements. Your job is to discuss the statement, decide if you agree or disagree with it, and find evidence to support your conclusion from the play. You can refer to the character's behaviour at certain points in the action and also collect some quotes spoken by your character that seem to prove your point.

Then choose one or two members of the group to report your findings to the whole class, making your arguments as convincing as possible. As each group reports back, the class awards points for good arguments.

The women in the play

Why do you think there are only two women in this play? Do you think the matter of who is to rule Rome has nothing to do with the women? Discuss these points as a whole class.

You will have noticed how very different the wives of Caesar and Brutus are, as presented in this play. Portia is strong-minded and insists on sharing in her husband's life – even in his worries – and she kills herself, by swallowing hot coals, when she knows he has been driven out of Rome. Calphurnia, on the other hand, seems to be ignored when she first appears and Caesar asks Antony to touch her in the race, to cure her barrenness, and her pleas for Caesar to stay away from the Capitol on the Ides of March are overruled.

Bring out this contrast by writing a profile of each of them. Work in pairs to discuss what you are going to put in your articles, and then write one of these each.

You can choose any point in the play for the article to appear – perhaps before Caesar's death for Calphurnia's, perhaps after Portia has killed herself for hers? Your profile of Portia could include your analysis of why she took this dreadful step.

Remember that we know Calphurnia has no children; we don't know about Portia. You can use a *little* imagination in making up some of the background details but don't confuse what you make up with what the play tells us.

Look at the character notes on page 69 to help you.

Make a wall display of the profiles of Portia and Calphurnia so that everyone can see what you have written.

Character jigsaw

Can you guess whose character these jigsaw pieces represent?

The answer, of course, is Brutus. Think of other pieces that might go to make up his whole personality. Copy the pieces above and add up to five more.

Divide into groups of about four or five and choose any character from the play: Antony, Cassius, Caesar, Octavius, Portia, Calphurnia, Casca, and Brutus are all good ones to choose.

Your task is to make up a picture of that character with little extracts from the play to show different aspects of them. In the group, decide which features of your chosen character you will work on. Each person in the group then takes one of your agreed features and hunts through the play for a short quotation that illustrates it.

For instance, Antony: one person chooses his love for Caesar and might find the line, 'That I did love thee, Caesar, O 'tis true' (Act 3 scene 1 line 194).

Another in the group chooses his clever public speaking, and finds a line (almost any one would do) from his speech to the citizens (Act 3 scene 2 lines 75–253).

When each person has found a line or two, put them all together into a presentation of your chosen character, with each of you speaking the lines you selected. The rest of the class can guess who the character is, and the aspects of that person you tried to convey.

Bystanders

There's a proverb which says, 'Onlookers see most of the game' – in other words, people who are not directly involved in an action can often notice more of what is going on.

Work in pairs. Choose a moment in the play when a certain character is an onlooker rather than a participant and make up the story of what that onlooker saw and heard.

Examples and suggestions

1 Popilius Lena is present early in Act 3 scene 1 when he speaks both to Cassius and to Caesar (lines 13–24). Imagine he watches what happens after that and think what he would report to his wife or friend afterwards.
2 The Soothsayer is also a witness at this time; he would be a good choice.
3 What story would the citizens tell after hearing the speeches of Brutus and Cassius in Act 3 scene 3? Choose just one individual.
4 Lucius, Brutus' servant, lets in the visitors in Act 2 scene 1. Perhaps he could have heard some of the conversation that followed? Imagine he has a mother who also works in the Brutus household and decide what he might tell her.
5 What story would one of Brutus' soldiers tell after Act 5 scene 5?

When you have worked out the outline of what might be said, use this to invent a short scene where the 'bystander' returns home and is questioned by their wife/husband/friend about what they saw and heard.

Show your scene to another pair and watch theirs.

Hot seat

Arrange chairs in a half circle if that is possible, with one special seat in front, facing the others.

Now find volunteers to take on the roles of Brutus, Antony, Cassius, and Caesar. Each of these characters may choose someone else to be his Personal Assistant or Publicity Manager who can sometimes answer on his behalf.

Each character now takes a turn in the special hot seat at the front, with the Publicity Manager standing behind him to help out when needed. While he is in that seat the character must answer in role the questions that the rest of the class put to him.

You will find that the most interesting questions are the ones about what the character thought or felt at certain points in the play and those about why he acted as he did. You will need to look at the character descriptions at the beginning of this section to help you to get under the skin of your character, and of course you will have to make up what you think he was feeling and what he was thinking. It is not always clear from the play just what is going on inside a character's mind.

The following suggestions may help you to prepare for your questions and for the answers.

1   *Brutus.* Look especially at his conversation with Cassius (Act 1 scene 2 lines 25–176) and at his soliloquy at the beginning of Act 2 scene 1.

    Questions should focus on why he joined the conspirators and what exactly he felt about Caesar.

2   *Antony.* The soliloquy after the conspirators have left in Act 3 scene 1 lines 254–275 is very important, as is the speech to the citizens in Act 3 scene 3.

    Questions could be about why he pretended to be friends with the conspirators and what his real plans were all the time.

3 *Cassius.* The scene with Brutus (Act 1 scene 2 lines 25–176) is vital to understanding him, and the final soliloquy at the very end of that scene, lines 308–322. Also consider the quarrel with Brutus in Act 4 scene 3 before the battle of Philippi.

Questions: ask him perhaps to justify his dishonest methods of persuasion. What does he feel about Caesar? What is his real opinion of his partner, Brutus?

4 *Caesar.* Look particularly at his reactions to his wife's dreams and the reassurances of the conspirators when they arrive in Act 2 scene 2. Also consider his refusal to listen to pleading for Publius Cimber in Act 3 scene 1 lines 35–77.

Questions: ask him about whether he really wanted to be king, and about his opinion of himself.

After about five or six questions and answers, change to a new character in the hot seat.

Afterwards, discuss as a class whether the characters might have answered as you did, and disagree with some of the answers others have given if you think they were wrong.

Plot

Staging posts

What would you pick out as the most important stages in the story that the play tells? What could be described as turning points?

See if you can complete this list, and add to it any other staging posts you think should be there.

1 Caesar's triumphant return to Rome.
2 Brutus joins Cassius' plot to kill Caesar.
3 The plot is almost foiled by ....
4 Caesar is assassinated.
5 Antony pretends to be friendly with ....
6 Speeches to the crowd by .... and ....
7 Violence grows: example? ....
8 .... flee from Rome.

9 Octavius joins Antony and .... to rule
   Rome.
10 Brutus and Cassius quarrel.
11 .... dies through a misunderstanding.
12 Brutus chooses .... rather than defeat.

Either divide these stages up among the members of the class and
each one of you draw a picture of an agreed size to show that
moment in the play. These can then be put together in a frieze
which tells the story of the play.

Or divide the class into small groups. Give out one staging post
to each group, which creates a freeze frame to show their bit of
action. Then show them one after another to tell the outline of
the whole play.

Ripple chart

What point would you pick as the climax of the action in this
play? You will probably pick the assassination of Caesar,
although that happens about halfway through and there's a lot of
play still to come after that.

Discuss with a partner what Shakespeare does to prevent the
audience feeling that the play is pretty well over after that. You'll
soon realize that he offers a very exciting and dramatic scene to
follow it. Even so, it is hard for a director to keep the interest of
an audience going throughout, and perhaps the best way to do so
is to emphasize the fact that everything that happens after
Caesar's death is a direct result of it – that Caesar is still there in
the background, pursuing his revenge.

First of all make a rough list of all the action that happens as a
consequence of the stabbing of Caesar:
1 Antony gets permission to speak in Caesar's funeral.
2 Brutus and Antony speak in turn to the citizens.
3 ....
and so on.

See if you can continue this list for yourselves.

Now think of the assassination as a pebble dropped in a pool,
and all the results of it as the ripples that move outwards from it.

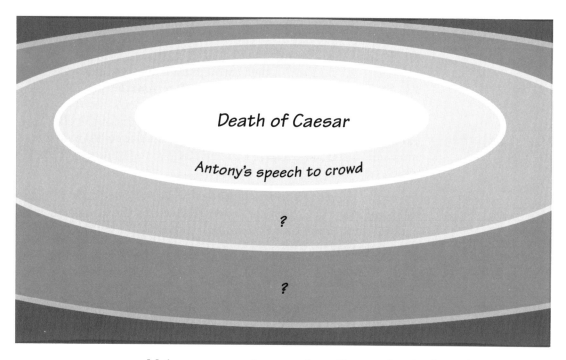

Death of Caesar

Antony's speech to crowd

?

?

Make your own chart on these lines and write into the ripples the various stages of the action that you listed. Put in as many ripples as you need, and put more than one event in the same ripple if you think it should be there.

When it's finished, the chart should show that the deaths of Brutus and Cassius are the final consequences for them of their action in stabbing Caesar.

Charting the fortunes of Brutus and Antony

Brutus' luck begins to run out as soon as he gives permission for Antony to speak at Caesar's funeral, though he doesn't realize it at the time.

Even at Philippi he still has hopes of victory, though his farewell to Cassius, Act 5 scene 1 lines 92–125, seems to show they both fear the worst.

As Antony's fortunes rise, so Brutus' and Cassius' fall. Try to chart this on a sort of graph, to show the high points and the low points of each of their fortunes, starting from Caesar's death.

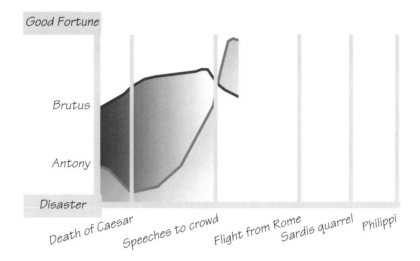

See if you can chart the rest of their fortunes.

Language and verse

Verse

The main verse form in this play, as in all Shakespeare's plays, is 'blank verse', or to give it its more formal label, 'iambic pentameter'. This is a five-beat line usually of ten syllables (sometimes an eleventh creeps in) in which the stresses alternate, as in this example:

> I come to bury Caesar, not to praise him.

(Stresses are marked by the symbol ⁄ above the syllable which is to be stressed.)

Blank verse does not rhyme, which means that it can be spoken against the beat and made to sound like ordinary speech.

Take the passage on page 80 as an example: work in pairs and read it through aloud first, taking alternate lines. Now do it again, tapping with your hand on the desk to mark the strong beats. Some of it is already marked for you with the stresses. See if you can work out where they come in the rest of it and mark them on a copy of the speech.

I have, when you have heard what I can say,
And know it now: the senate have concluded
To give this day a crown to mighty Caesar.
If you shall send them word you will not come,
Their minds may change. Besides, it were a mock
Apt to be render'd, for some one to say
'Break up the senate to another time,
When Caesar's wife shall meet with better dreams'.

Try your own blank verse

You'll find that the basic pattern of alternate strong and weak beats is so natural to ordinary speech that it isn't hard to speak in blank verse deliberately.

Try a conversation with a partner. You could start with:

It's easy when you have the knack, I say.

or:

Blank verse makes all this sound important, now.

Missing punctuation

Another way of exploring the rhythms of the verse is to work on an extract which has had most of the punctuation removed.

Look at this:

But I am constant as the northern star
Of whose true-fix'd and resting quality
There is no fellow in the firmament
The skies are painted with unnumber'd sparks
They are all fire and every one doth shine
But there's but one in all doth hold his place
So in the world 'tis furnish'd well with men
And men are flesh and blood and apprehensive
Yet in the number I do know but one
That unassailable holds on his rank
Unshak'd of motion and that I am he
Let me a little show it even in this
That I was constant Cimber should be banish'd
And constant do remain to keep him so.

Read it through first and see if you can divide it up into sentences.

When you have done this, divide into groups of five or six, and sit in a circle. In turn round the circle, read the speech, taking one 'sense unit' each (that is a section which would usually be marked off by a full stop, semicolon, or colon, or by 'and' or a similar word.) When you have got to the end, read round again, this time taking one line each but keeping the sense going at the same time. Don't let your voice drop at the end of your line if the meaning goes on – your tone should be picked up by the person reading the next line. Have several goes at this if you need to.

Try to listen as well as read: you should hear that there are two rhythms going on at the same time: the normal sentence rhythm and the blank verse.

More missing punctuation

The lines of the next piece of verse have been run in together, so it looks like prose. Work in pairs to see if you can puzzle out where the lines, and the sentences, end. First, make a rough draft each, putting the words into lines; then compare notes and discuss any variations. Finally make a fair copy of your answer in lines.

> I know where I will wear this dagger then Cassius from bondage will deliver Cassius therein ye gods you make the weak most strong therein ye gods you tyrants do defeat nor stony tower nor walls of beaten brass nor airless dungeon nor strong links of iron can be retentive to the strength of spirit but life being weary of these worldly bars never lacks power to dismiss itself.

(Remember that as a rule, each line should have ten syllables.)

The lines are not all regular, but most of them have about ten syllables and most follow the usual blank verse pattern.

When you've tried to sort out the lines, compare your version with the speech in the play: Act 1 scene 3 lines 89–97.

Prose

Keep in the same pairs.

There are certain things that Shakespeare writes in prose – with no regular beat or rhythm except the usual rhythms of spoken English. One of these is letters – they stand out from the rest of the play because they are not in blank verse. Can you remember any letters in this play? Look for them.

Another use of prose is in any conversation which is meant to sound rather uneducated. Humble characters often speak prose in Shakespeare's plays.

To see this at work, turn to the opening scene of the play. Which characters speak in prose and which in verse here? Work out why this is.

Look at the prose in the other 'crowd scenes' in the play – Act 3 scenes 2 and 3. Write down a few lines about what you noticed, and compare what you found out with the rest of the class.

Did you find any letters in prose? The one Brutus receives from an anonymous citizen (really written by Cassius) is too short for you to see if it is prose, but Artemidorus' warning to Caesar in Act 2 scene 3 is a better example.

Themes and ideas

Setting . . . past or present?

In Shakespeare's day, very little attention was paid to realistic setting or costume. Often the actors wore everyday clothes (doublet and hose, or long gowns for old men and women) with just a symbolic extra touch to suggest the time or place, like a crown, cloak or, in the case of Julius Caesar, a laurel wreath. There is a very unusual sketch of a group of Elizabethan actors performing Shakespeare's play *Titus Andronicus* dressed in togas, but most of the time actors would have worn their own clothes.

So if a director of a modern production wants to recapture something of the time in which the play was written, he or she can dress the cast in Elizabethan clothes throughout. More often, the play is set in the Roman period and the actors wear togas and tunics. Sometimes, however, the director decides to make the play seem to have a special meaning for our own time and then modern dress is the obvious choice. Some of the most striking productions of our own century have been modern-dress ones, and one very famous production in 1936 by Orson Welles used modern military uniforms very like those worn by Hitler's followers in Germany at that time. Here is a photo of Caesar in that production looking quite like Hitler himself.

Can you see what effect this might have? Think about where the audience's sympathies might be in such a production. Whose side would they tend to be on?

Costume designs

Now imagine you are to direct a production and think about what effect you want to achieve: design costumes for a few of the main characters. If you decide on togas, you will need to do a little research in your library to find out who wore what in ancient Rome. If you want to dress your actors in Elizabethan clothes and try to recapture the flavour of a production of Shakespeare's day, then you will also need to do some research. Use books on the history of costume to see what was worn in the late sixteenth century. Don't get too carried away by historical accuracy, though, as costumes to suit the characters and their rank and age group are even more important.

If you like the idea of a modern setting, think what country or area you wish to set it in – maybe a country with a military-style ruler and Secret Police? Or what about a future setting? That would give scope for fantastic costumes and would still allow you to make a political point.

Science fiction often shows future societies in order to make some point about our own by its parallels (as *Star Trek* often does) so your future setting could allow you to criticize Caesar as a potential dictator or to show the conspirators as terrorists.

Make some sketches of your designs, each labelled with the name of the character and with a few notes about why you chose this outfit for this person. Display them afterwards for everyone to see and discuss.

Stage props

Which actor in the play needs a book as a prop? (If you can't remember, look up Act 4 scene 3 line 251.)

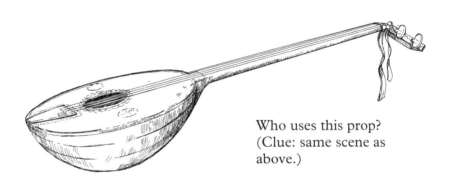

Who uses this prop? (Clue: same scene as above.)

Can you think of any other props that are used in the play? If you were A.S.M. (Assistant Stage Manager) of a production, one of your jobs would be to check the props table before each performance to see that all the 'personal props' (those carried by the actors, not set on the stage) are ready to hand.

There would be a wine flask and 'cups' on the table: who would be using them? (See Act 4 scene 3 line 156.)

Who needs a letter or document to read from and offer to Caesar? (See Act 2 scene 3.)

Who uses a cloak with slits in it? (See Act 3 scene 2 line 171.)

There would certainly be some daggers on the props table – can you remember who would use them?

Some props are not actually mentioned in the lines of the play, like the daggers, but are needed in the action. There would also be some things on the props table that the director or the actor concerned thinks will help to create the character – like money for Cassius to chink at times, perhaps, to indicate the 'itching palm' that Brutus speaks of?

Props quiz

Take any character you like and choose a prop for him or her – either one that needs to be used in the action or one which stands for an aspect of his or her personality. Draw your chosen prop. Number the drawings and put them up on the wall. The class then tries to guess which character each prop is meant for.

The language of the play: poster quotes

Look carefully at the ten quotations from the play on pages 88–89. All of them create a vivid picture in the mind.

They all have at least one thing in common: each of them offers a visual picture. That means they are all *images* – examples of metaphorical language in which the speaker imagines a striking comparison.

Your task is to choose one or two of them and draw a picture (or cut scraps from magazines to make a collage) of the image the line creates for you. Then write the chosen line on top of your picture, to make a kind of poster. You may have seen poems on posters, or in poetry books, that have a drawing backing the printed words of the poem – this is the kind of thing you should aim at.

For instance: take the 'dogs of war'. You might draw some fierce and vicious dogs, straining to be let off the lead, perhaps with some military touch about them like helmets, and write the words over the top of the picture in very distinct letters.

1

'Why, man, he doth bestride the narrow world
Like a Colossus; and we petty men
Walk under his huge legs, and peep about
To find ourselves dishonourable graves.'
Act 1 scene 2 lines 134–137

Cassius speaking of Caesar's domination of Rome.
Colossus was an ancient statue in Rhodes – of huge size.

2

'Think him as a serpent's egg
Which, hatch'd, would, as his kind, grow mischievous,
And kill him in the shell.'
Act 2 scene 1 lines 32–34

Brutus, on the threat Caesar poses to Rome if he is not stopped.

3

'It is the bright day that brings forth the adder.'
Act 2 scene 1 line 14

Brutus again, on the hidden danger of Caesar.

4

'I am constant as the northern star.'
Act 3 scene 1 line 60

Caesar of himself.

5

'Here wast thou bay'd, brave hart;
Here didst thou fall; and here thy hunters stand.'
Act 3 scene 1 lines 204–205

Antony, looking at dead Caesar, thinks him like a hunted deer.

6

'. . . let slip the dogs of war.'

Act 3 scene 1 line 273

Antony, on the revenge he seeks for Caesar's murder.

7

'I had rather be a dog, and bay the moon,
Than such a Roman.'

Act 4 scene 3 lines 27–28

Brutus to Cassius, during their quarrel.

8

'O Cassius, you are yoked with a lamb
That carries anger as the flint bears fire,
Who, much enforced, shows a hasty spark,
And straight is cold again.'

Act 4 scene 3 lines 109–112

Brutus sees himself as difficult to anger, like a flint which can produce a spark but quickly cools.

9

'There is a tide in the affairs of men
Which, taken at the flood, leads on to fortune.'

Act 4 scene 3 lines 217–218

Brutus about their chances in battle.

10

'A peevish schoolboy, worthless of such honour.'

Act 5 scene 1 line 61

Cassius about Octavius.

Image search

Give one act of the play to each of five groups. Each group skims through its act to find any striking images. (Remember these are examples of imaginative language which conjure up a picture in the mind.) As you find them, sort them into groups:

1   comparisons of people with animals
2   warlike images – to do with armies, fighting, etc., and weapons
3   any other notable ones which do not fall into these two categories.

When you have collected together all the images in your act that come under these headings, take a large sheet of paper and put it on the wall. Write up the quotes grouped in three sets – labelled 'Animals', 'War and Violence' and 'Others'. Finally look at the other groups' work and compare their findings with yours. Discuss any conclusions you come to as a class.

Follow-up

If you had to find one single image to sum up your idea of the play *Julius Caesar*, what would it be? The body of Caesar stained with blood? Or just a bloodstained dagger? Or perhaps the storm? Or even the northern star? See what you can think of and talk about your ideas with a partner. Now, on your own, choose one image to include in a design for a programme cover or a handbill for an imaginary production. Add any necessary information about date, time, and venue of the play.

Display the finished programme designs, together with the poster quotes, and share your ideas with the rest of the class.

Themes: politics

Imagine that two political parties are competing in an election for the votes of Romans. Brutus is supported by Cassius and Antony is Campaign Manager for Caesar.

These four people have been invited onto the panel for a *Question Time* programme. Choose members of the class to take on these four roles, plus one to be the Chair to keep order in the discussion. The rest of you are the audience who can ask

ELECTION MANIFESTO:

THE IMPERIAL PARTY

We see the future of Rome as a monarchy.

Decision-making will be much faster and more efficient with all the government in the hands of one man, who will control the army, organize defence, and make the laws by which the citizens will live.

Law and order will be high on our agenda and no traitors and undesirables will be permitted to spread revolutionary ideas among the populace.

Rome will be famous throughout the world as a great power and our influence will spread even further than it does at present.

STRONG GOVERNMENT IS WHAT WE NEED.

Our candidate is a brave soldier and a man popular with the ordinary people.

VOTE IMPERIAL! VOTE CAESAR!

For a better future!

Election manifesto:

the FREEDOM PARTY

Keep Rome free!

We will ensure that the rights of Romans are preserved. All laws will be made by the representatives of the citizens of Rome and not by the whims of a single man.

Justice is the right of every Roman and we will see it is available to all. Our ancestors fought in the past to avoid being ruled by a king or a dictator and we owe it to them to continue this fight.

Our candidate is a man of the highest qualities – honest and respected, just and honourable.

Vote Freedom! Vote Brutus!

Keep your Roman rights!

questions and also give your own opinions briefly when asked by the Chair.

First, whether you are panel member or audience, you will need to study carefully the two manifestos on page 91 and note down what you want to say. (Perhaps your teacher would agree to be Chair if there isn't anyone willing and able to do it. One of the important decisions to be made by the Chair is when to move on to the next question.)

Follow-up

Work in pairs. Decide which party you are going to support and then write some election leaflets for your side. These are to be delivered to the houses of the Roman citizens. No one will read them if they are too long-winded, so keep them snappy. Use suitable slogans and above all get the candidate's name, character and background over to the voters.

The crowd

In Act 1 scene 1, the citizens are in holiday mood, laughing and joking with the Tribunes and eager to celebrate Caesar's victory until they realize they shouldn't be. They are quite easily convinced, though, aren't they? This gives a hint that they are fickle and easily swayed, which prepares the audience for what happens later.

In Act 1 scene 2 the citizens don't appear but Casca speaks about the offer of the crown to Caesar and how the citizens cheered at his refusal. Look up these reports again (lines 233–287) and find at least one quotation which shows how sympathetic they were when he fell down in an epileptic fit, and write it down.

The next time a crowd of citizens takes an active part in the play is after Caesar's death when first Brutus and then Antony speaks to them in the Forum (Act 3 scene 2). Remind yourselves of how they react to Brutus (lines 49–73) and then how they are swayed by Antony in the rest of this scene. Choose and write down another quotation for each of these points.

By the end of this scene they are out for the conspirators' blood and the incident with Cinna the poet (Act 3 scene 3) shows just how far the violence has spread. Pick just one more line to remind you of this senseless attack.

TV newscast

To prepare for this, discuss with a partner what idea of the behaviour of crowds the play appears to be showing. Do you agree that when a crowd gets worked up it can begin to behave in a way the individuals in it would never behave on their own? See if you can think of any examples from modern life. What about vandalism by crowds of youngsters? Or football 'hooligans'? Have you ever seen rioters on TV breaking up shop windows or overturning cars?

Bring your ideas to a class discussion.

Now work in small groups of three or four and put together a TV newscast for the day after Caesar's assassination. You can assume that the actual events of Caesar's death were covered the night before. Your newscast only needs to deal with the aftermath. Concentrate on the breakdown of law and order that was seen in the killing of Cinna the poet, and imagine other such incidents happening all over Rome. You could include an interview with a police chief who could give a report on how public order is being restored. The Triumvirate has taken over rule in Rome (see work on Act 4 scene 1) and a spokesman for them could give you another interview. Add your own reports sent in by reporters from various parts of the city, who will tell you of the flight of the conspirators from Rome and the mood of Rome as Caesar is being buried. Use your own ideas to make it seem as realistic a broadcast as you can and put on a performance for the rest of the class.

Whose tragedy?

In everyday life the word 'tragedy' is used to mean any kind of disaster, like a road accident or the death of someone in a bomb incident, but in Shakespeare's theatre it had a special meaning. It was used about a play which shows the downfall of a man looked up to as a hero, but who is not perfect. He is neither wholly good nor wholly bad. He mustn't be completely wicked or the audience will not feel any sympathy for him and won't care what happens to him; he mustn't be totally good or his downfall will be just too upsetting and painful, and unbelievable.

This play is rather different from any other Shakespeare play in that it isn't really clear whose tragedy is being shown – is it Caesar's or Brutus'?

Work in pairs. One of you work on Caesar and the other work on Brutus. Write down the good and the bad things about your character in two columns. Share your ideas with your partner, and discuss which character fits the role of tragic hero better. Bear in mind another factor as you consider this: whose story seems most interesting to the audience? Whom do they care most about?

Bring your answers to a general class discussion on this topic. There is no right answer to be found – it is all a matter of opinion.

Guilty!

Who do you think was most responsible for Caesar's death?

Perhaps you think Cassius must bear most of the blame because of his plotting and scheming to get all the conspirators together and his persuasion of Brutus to join them?

Or was it Brutus, the respected senator who lent his name and his support to the plot and in doing so betrayed his friend?

You could argue that Caesar himself was the guilty one, in his ambition to become king, and his arrogance towards everyone else. Did he bring it all on himself?

Try to settle the question by setting up a coroner's court – a heavenly one, so that you can call dead people as witnesses if you wish. A coroner is the person, rather like a judge, who has to decide in his court how a person died and if anyone else was responsible.

Get your teacher to choose two or three people to be the coroners, then divide the rest of the class into three main groups. Each group draws lots to see which of the three possible culprits is the one they are going to accuse.

The task of each group is to be thoroughly biased – to put the case against their character, whatever they may really believe. To do so, each group needs at least one counsel for the prosecution, plus characters from the play to be called as witnesses – and, of course, one person to be the accused. This is the only one who tries to defend himself against the rest of the group, as he is questioned by the prosecution.

You can also prepare some evidence to support your case, which can be in the form of freeze frames prepared by anyone else in the group who is not needed as a witness or lawyer. These should show moments from the action of the play that indicate the guilt of your character.

This will need a lot of planning and below there are some notes and ideas to help you.

While the counsel for the prosecution are working on their cases, the coroners should prepare questions they want to ask each of the accused. They can also get the room ready, making it as much like a courtroom as possible.

The case against Caesar

Witnesses:

Marullus and Flavius to say how he came back to Rome and was worshipped by the citizens.
Casca to tell about the offer of the crown and how Caesar really wanted it all the time.
Decius to say how he got Caesar to go to the Capitol.
Brutus to tell of his fears about Caesar.

Freeze frames:

- of his procession into Rome after defeating Pompey
- of Antony offering a crown
- of his arrogant behaviour over Publius Cimber.

The case against Cassius

Witnesses:

Antony to tell what Caesar thought of Cassius.
A servant to say how he forged letters from citizens to Brutus.
One of the conspirators to say he wanted to kill Antony as well.

Freeze frames:

- of his persuasion of Brutus
- of his persuasion of Casca
- of his stories about Caesar.

The case against Brutus

Witnesses:

Antony to say how upset Caesar must have been at his friend's betrayal.

His servant Lucius to tell about the visit of the conspirators to their house.

One of the conspirators to say how many mistakes he made, like sparing Antony.

Freeze frames:

- of his welcoming the conspirators into his house
- of his stabbing Caesar and Caesar's sense of betrayal
- of his speech to the citizens.

Add to these ideas any more you can think of. Give each group a time limit of five minutes to present its case. After the coroners have heard and seen all the evidence they must decide on their verdict and announce it to the class.